Religions of the Axial Age: An Approach to the World's Religions

Part I

Professor Mark W. Muesse

THE TEACHING COMPANY ®

PUBLISHED BY:

THE TEACHING COMPANY
4151 Lafayette Center Drive, Suite 100
Chantilly, Virginia 20151-1232
1-800-TEACH-12
Fax—703-378-3819
www.teach12.com

Printed in the United States of America

ISBN 1-59803-283-6

Mark W. Muesse, Ph.D.

Chair of the Department of Religious Studies, Rhodes College

Mark W. Muesse is the Chair of the Department of Religious Studies at Rhodes College in Memphis, Tennessee. He received a B.A., *summa cum laude*, in English Literature from Baylor University and earned a Master of Theological Studies, a Master of Arts, and a Ph.D. in the Study of Religion from Harvard University.

Prior to taking his position at Rhodes, Professor Muesse held positions at Harvard College, Harvard Divinity School, and the University of Southern Maine, where he served as Associate Dean of the College of Arts and Sciences.

Professor Muesse is the author of many articles, papers, and reviews in world religions, spirituality, theology, and gender studies and has co-edited a collection of essays entitled *Redeeming Men: Religion and Masculinities*. He is currently compiling an anthology of prayers from around the world.

Professor Muesse is a member of the American Academy of Religion and the Society for Indian Philosophy and Religion and has been a visiting professor at the Tamilnadu Theological Seminary in Madurai, India. He has traveled extensively throughout Asia and has studied at Wat Mahadhatu, Bangkok, Thailand; the Himalayan Yogic Institute, Kathmandu, Nepal; the Subodhi Institute of Integral Education in Sri Lanka; and Middle East Technical University in Ankara, Turkey.

Professor Muesse and his wife, Dhammika, have a daughter, Ariyana. For The Teaching Company, he has also taught *Great World Religions: Hinduism*.

Acknowledgments: I gratefully acknowledge the assistance of the following individuals in preparing this course: my friend Dr. Manoj Jain, who helped me with the lecture on Jainism; my editorial assistant Mr. Michael Turco, who ably assisted with the written elements; Dr. Joan Burton, The Teaching Company's Academic Content Supervisor for this course; and most especially, my wife, Dr. Dhammika Swarnamali Muesse, who has deepened my understanding of Buddhism and supported me in every phase of this project.

Table of Contents
Religions of the Axial Age: An Approach to the World's Religions
Part I

Religions of the Axial Age:
An Approach to the World's Religions

Scope:

The years 800–200 B.C.E. comprise one of the most creative and influential eras in world history. The German philosopher Karl Jaspers termed this epoch *die Achsenzeit*, or the Axial Age, to indicate its pivotal importance in the evolution of human thought. Around the globe, sages and moralists, philosophers and priests grappled with novel ideas about the nature of humanity, the world, and ultimate reality and approached these issues with fresh ways of thinking. Of such importance was this era that modern people continue to live out their moral and religious lives through the fundamental categories and patterns of thought established during this time.

The ferment of religious and philosophical activity centered in four distinct regions of civilization: East Asia, South Asia, West Asia, and the northeastern Mediterranean. Each of these areas witnessed the emergence of several imaginative individuals whose exemplary lives and teachings prompted their followers to create the traditions that led to the birth of the world religions. By setting these traditions and thinkers in juxtaposition, we are able to see more clearly the nature of the questions with which they struggled and to appreciate the similarities and differences of their solutions. We can also understand how their ideas have determined theological and religious thought and practices down to our day.

The course begins with a discussion of the idea of the Axial Age and its characteristics and contours. The introductory lecture accents the importance of this period and explains the value of studying religions comparatively across a specific period of time, rather than merely as traditions isolated from one another and unrelated to larger developments in the evolution of the human spirit. Although the Axial Age had an impact on four major regions, this course will attend principally to the three Asian sites, primarily because of their importance in shaping the world religions and because The Teaching Company already offers a number of excellent courses devoted to the world of the ancient Greeks. In this series, we will focus on the developments of Zoroastrianism in Iran and its influence on Judaism,

Christianity, and Islam; Hinduism, Buddhism, and Jainism in India; and Confucianism and Daoism in China. The course will unfold regionally, beginning in Central Asia, then tracing developments in West Asia, South Asia, and finally, East Asia.

Although it is not an Axial center, we begin in Central Asia to study the early Indo-European peoples, who later migrated to West and South Asia and decisively shaped the religious outlook and practices of those regions. We will examine the shared culture of a group of these Central Asians known today as the *Indo-Iranians* and explore their similarities and differences after they divide in the second millennium B.C.E. When we get to West Asia, particularly ancient Iran, we examine the context out of which came perhaps the most mysterious of all major Axial sages: Zoroaster, also known as Zarathustra. Zoroaster, who may have been the world's first prophet, was responsible for reforming the ancient Iranian religious tradition and for numerous theological innovations, such as the apocalyptic Day of Judgment, the devil, and perhaps even the idea of a messiah or savior. We will look at these new conceptions both in their native Iranian context and as possible influences on Judaism, Christianity, and Islam.

In South Asia, we start with the indigenous Indus culture and witness the impact of the migration of the branch of the Indo-Iranians (retrospectively called the Indo-Aryans) that eventually made its way to northwestern India. We explore the elements of both Indus and Indo-Aryan religions to prepare for the examination of the Axial transformation of Indian religion. Pre-Axial religion in India focused on this-worldly concerns, such as the acquisition of material needs and comforts, long life, and successful reproduction, and was decidedly oriented toward ritual. With the advent of the Axial Age, Indian sages began to question the values associated with the material world and ritual practices. Indian religion became increasingly preoccupied with understanding the destiny of the individual and the nature of the deepest reality underlying all appearances. After a great deal of speculation, the ideas of reincarnation and karma were widely accepted, creating a new problem for Indian religion: attaining release from the endless rounds of death and rebirth known as *samsara*. Individuals by the hundreds began to renounce worldly life and experiment with solutions to this predicament. Among the scores of new spiritualities developed during this time, we examine three of the most important and most enduring: the mysticism of the Upanishads, which provided the foundational structure for the massive conglomerate of religious beliefs and practices later known as Hinduism; the teachings of the Buddha, based on an approach he called the Middle Way; and the beliefs and practices of the Mahavira, whose movement became known as Jainism. Setting these traditions side by side will afford us the chance to see how they responded to many of the same problems but offered distinctive and innovative solutions.

Our final destination is East Asia. We begin with a study of the pre-Axial culture of what will later become China. Understanding this early period, which is barely within reach of current historiography, is important to appreciate the Axial transformations brought about by Confucius and thinkers associated with the tradition of Daoism. We look at the earliest attestations of religious practices that have been important throughout Chinese history, including divination and ancestor reverence. Later, when we turn to Confucius and his followers and then to the Daoists, we observe how these practices are retained and reinterpreted to fit the new concern with moral behavior brought by the Axial Age. Claiming only to transmit ancient traditions, Confucius taught a comprehensive ethic of personal development that remained influential throughout Chinese history and provided the basis for the Chinese educational system. Daoism, often associated with the mythic figure of Laozi, was concerned with many of the same issues as Confucius but suggested other solutions. Throughout Chinese history, Confucianism and Daoism functioned as complements to each other in such a way that individuals could claim allegiance to both Daoist and Confucian traditions.

The series concludes with a set of reflections on the Axial transformations, emphasizing both the common themes across the centers of development and their distinctive qualities. We will consider the overall significance of this age for human history and its major contributions to human spirituality.

Lecture One
What Was the Axial Age?

Scope:

The Axial Age refers to the period of time from approximately 800–200 B.C.E., in which unprecedented developments occurred in four separate centers of civilization: West Asia, South Asia, East Asia, and the northeastern Mediterranean. Just the mention of some of the individuals who lived during this period in these localities alerts us to the importance of the age: Zoroaster, Jeremiah, Isaiah, the Buddha, Vardhamana Mahavira, Confucius, Pythagoras, Heraclitus, Socrates, Plato, and Aristotle. In different ways, these individuals responded to an array of new issues stirred up by increased urbanization, political instability, the emergence of self-consciousness, and the impulse to understand the world and the human place in it as comprehensively as possible. These social and intellectual dynamics led to intense reflection on the nature and destiny of the individual, the fundamental questions of morality, and the character of ultimate reality. As a consequence of their creative engagement with these issues, the sages of the Axial Age produced the intellectual and moral matrix out of which the world's religions were born; subsequent religious developments are, in large measure, the developments of the ideas and insights from the Axial period.

Outline

I. The Axial Age, the period between 800 and 200 B.C.E., saw a remarkable burst of creativity almost simultaneously in four separate areas of the Eurasian continent.

- **A.** In East Asia, in the area we now call China, Confucius and his followers provided the religious, philosophical, and political foundations for more than 2,000 years of Chinese culture. At the same time, Daoist philosophers produced a compelling alternative to Confucianism.
- **B.** In South Asia, a countercultural movement of ascetics and mystics composed a collection of teachings called the Upanishads that gave nascent Hinduism its characteristic features. Near the same time and place, both the Buddha and

Mahavira attained new insights that inaugurated Buddhism and Jainism.

C. In West Asia, in Palestine, the prophets of Judah helped shape the emerging religion of Judaism. Also in West Asia, in Iran, Zarathustra had recently established Zoroastrianism, which served as the state religion of three powerful empires and contributed decisive new ideas to Judaism and Christianity.

D. Finally, in the northern Mediterranean, in the land of ancient Greece, Thales, Pythagoras, Heraclitus, Socrates, Plato, and Aristotle essentially invented the Western philosophical tradition.

E. Just as fascinating as the density of genius in this era is the similarity of ideas and modes of thinking that these individuals developed. They all struggled with many of the same fundamental issues, such as the nature and destiny of the self, the basis and practices of morality, and the highest goods of human life.

II. The 20th-century German philosopher Karl Jaspers (1883–1969) identified this extraordinary period as *die Achsenzeit*, or the Axial Age, signifying that this era was pivotal in human history.

A. During the Axial Age, as Jaspers observed, "The spiritual foundations of humanity were laid simultaneously and independently... And these are the foundations upon which humanity still subsists today."

B. What was happening at this particular time and in these particular places that might account for the prodigious output of critical ideas and the appearance of some of the greatest individuals known to the world?

III. We can point to several social and political developments that contributed to the opening of the Axial Age.

A. The Axial era occurred at a time and in places of increasing urbanization and mobility. This trend had significant effects on social structures and the human psyche. Urban life often disrupts one's sense of identity and places traditional values and beliefs in doubt.

B. Second, the Axial centers were generally characterized by political and legal upheaval.

1. The Chinese Axial Age, for example, overlapped a brutal epoch in Chinese history known as the Period of Warring States. India, Judah, and Iran underwent similar periods of turmoil and transformation.
2. Rapid political and social change, of course, generates uncertainty and insecurity, but interestingly, such times are often the most creative and innovative for religious and philosophical thought.

C. Sages in all the Axial centers became increasingly anxious about death and preoccupied with what, if anything, lay beyond death.

1. Pre-Axial humans, of course, were not unconcerned with death, but their sense of identity was more firmly rooted in their participation in the family, clan, or tribe. Accordingly, death could be accepted, knowing that the family would survive one's personal demise.
2. By the Axial Age, attitudes toward death began to reflect a greater concern about the experience of dying and the afterlife. Increasingly, death was regarded with dread, and speculation about what might lie beyond was filled with both hope and terror.
3. Reflected in this shift in attitudes about death is the rise of a sense of individuality and a greater consciousness of the human being as a moral agent, accountable for his or her own actions.
4. As humans began to think of themselves as separate, autonomous individuals, death became a more dreadful reality. Selfhood promotes a feeling of isolation or, at least, differentiation from the rest of the human community and the rest of reality, making it more difficult to accept dying as part of the natural process of living.

D. The growing sense of selfhood and anxiety about life's transience also stimulated conjectures about the nature of the person and spurred the search to discover something within the human individual that might endure the dissolution of the body, something eternal or immortal.

1. As part of this quest, Axial sages developed a new way of thinking about the world and the place of humanity in it. S. N. Eisenstadt, one of the first scholars to study the sociological dimensions of the Axial Age, calls this way of looking at life *transcendental consciousness*, that is, the ability to stand back and see the world more comprehensively and critically.
2. Transcendental consciousness produced novel conceptions of the world's ultimate reality. In some cases, the Axial sages were not content to accept the old anthropomorphic gods and goddesses as the highest realities or powers governing the universe. They imagined sublime conceptions of ultimate reality, such as the Hindu Brahman and the Chinese Dao.
3. Thinking about the highest realities also led these individuals to a greater interest in *epistemology*, that is, how we know what we know and what the limitations of our knowledge are. Attention to epistemology, accordingly, promoted a greater sense of self-consciousness and awareness of humanity's place in the universe.

E. Finally, the Axial Age marks a dramatic change in the very function of religion in human life. During this era, the purpose of religion shifted from what theologian John Hick calls *cosmic maintenance* to *personal transformation.*
1. By *cosmic maintenance*, we mean that religion functions chiefly as a ritual means for human beings to collaborate with the divine powers to assist in keeping the world in good working order.
2. During the Axial Age, however, religion takes on an unprecedented new role in human life: providing the means for the individual to undergo change in order to achieve immortality or happiness.
3. Selfhood and the heightened awareness of suffering and death prompted some religions to imagine wonderful afterlife experiences as ways to overcome the painful realities of this life. Reaching these goals might mean accepting a new vision of the way the world works or accepting the demands of a particular god with the power to bestow immortality or paradise.

- **F.** Jaspers was certainly correct in his contention that this era laid contemporary humanity's spiritual foundations. In these lectures, we will probe this idea in greater detail by examining developments in the Axial centers in West, South, and East Asia. For those interested in Axial Age developments in Greece and Judah, I recommend The Teaching Company courses in Greek philosophy and Judaism.

IV. The approach of this course is unlike that of many courses in comparative or world religions.

- **A.** Some courses in religion focus on a particular tradition, such as Islam or Christianity, approaching the material in a chronological fashion. This method allows one to study a single religious tradition in depth and shows how religions evolve over time.
- **B.** In the second general method of religious studies, students examine religions one by one, noting similarities and differences. This method allows comparisons of various traditions, but the treatment is often shallow, and historical development is glossed over. Further, the short time allotted to each tradition often means that the religion's development in the larger context of its culture is neglected, as are the ways in which one religious tradition shapes others.
- **C.** By examining these religions over the 600-year span of the Axial Age and against the background of their pre-Axial settings, we will have the opportunity to study religions both in their historical development *and* comparatively.
  1. The comparative dimension allows us to view how different religions respond to similar historical and sociological circumstances. It also allows us to see the mutual interaction of religions in proximity to one another.
  2. Limiting the time frame and the number of religions we cover enables us to gain a measure of depth in our investigation and connect the religions more fully with their social and political contexts.
  3. The greatest value of this course, however, derives from the era on which it is focused. The Axial Age is simply one of the most intriguing periods in religious history.

We are about to observe the world's great religions coming to life.

Essential Reading:

Jaspers, *The Origin and Goal of History*, part 1, chapters 1–4.

Supplementary Reading:

Eisenstadt, *The Origins and Diversity of Axial Age Civilizations*, Introduction.

Hick, *An Interpretation of Religion*, chapter 2.

Questions to Consider:

1. Are there other historical periods that compare with the creativity and influence of the Axial Age?
2. The Axial Age seems to emerge in connection with human self-consciousness. What may account for the rise of self-consciousness?

Lecture One—Transcript
What Was the Axial Age?

The middle of the first millennium B.C.E. was one of the most astonishing times in the history of humanity. Between 800 and 200 B.C.E., there appeared a cohort of brilliant individuals whose teachings left deep—and perhaps indelible—impressions on the way human beings thought about themselves and the world around them. And today, we are still living out, and living through, the ideas and ideals that were introduced in this period.

Remarkably, this burst of creativity occurred almost simultaneously in four separate areas of the Eurasian continent. In East Asia, in the area that we now call China, Confucius and his followers provided the religious, philosophical, and political foundations for over 2,000 years of Chinese culture. At the same time, Daoist philosophers produced a compelling alternative to Confucianism, impacting Chinese culture in an equally powerful but very different way. In South Asia, a countercultural movement of ascetics and mystics composed a collection of profound teachings called the *Upanishads* that gave nascent Hinduism its characteristic features. Near the same time and place, both the Buddha and the Mahavira attained new insights that inaugurated Buddhism, the first major international religion, and Jainism, a small but highly influential Indian religion. In West Asia, in Palestine, the prophets of Judah—such as Jeremiah and Second Isaiah—helped shape the emerging religion of Judaism, which had just begun to assume its' distinctive qualities. In West Asia, in the land of Iran, Zoroaster had recently established Zoroastrianism, which served as the state religion of three powerful empires and contributed decisive new ideas to Judaism and Christianity. Finally, in the northern Mediterranean region in the land of ancient Greece, Thales, Pythagoras, Heraklitus, Socrates, Plato, and Aristotle essentially invented the Western philosophical tradition.

Rarely in human history do we find such a dense concentration of creative individuals in such a short period of time, especially individuals whose lives and teachings have had such an extensive and long-lasting impact. But just as fascinating as the density of genius in this era, is the similarity of ideas and modes of thinking that these individuals developed—despite their geographical distance from one another. Although they did not always come to the same conclusions or advocate the same practices and beliefs, they struggled with many of the same fundamental issues, such as the nature and destiny of the self, the basis and practices of morality, and the highest goods of human life.

The 20th-century German philosopher Karl Jaspers identified this extraordinary period as *die Achsenzeit*, or the Axial Age. By choosing this name, Jaspers signified that this era was pivotal in human history, demarcating a decisive change between what came before and what came afterwards. During the Axial Age, as Jaspers eloquently put it, "The spiritual foundations of humanity were laid simultaneously and independently... And these are the foundations upon which humanity still subsists today."

What was going on here? What was happening at this particular time and in these particular places that might account for the prodigious output of critical ideas and the appearance of some of the greatest individuals known to the world? To begin to answer this weighty question, let me discuss a series of social and political developments that were occurring in these Axial centers during this period.

First, the Axial era occurred at a time and in places of increasing urbanization. More and more, people were living in closer proximity to one another, in towns and cities. People, of course, lived in urban settings prior to Axial Age, but now that practice accelerated and expanded. Previously nomadic peoples began to settle down and to take up agriculture and enjoy the benefits of more sedentary existence. Those who had lived in villages moved to larger towns and cities to take advantage of new economic opportunities that awaited them.

Urbanization was significant because of its effects on social structures and on the human psyche. Urban life often disrupts one's sense of identity and places traditional beliefs and values in doubt. In towns and cities, one often meets others quite unlike oneself, and that fact frequently challenges a person to look at himself or herself in very different ways. Conventional beliefs and ways of being are thrown into flux. Some persons are challenged by such conditions to entertain new ideas, while others cling more steadfastly to their old ones. In either case, customs and tradition often lose their taken-for-granted character. Higher concentrations of persons also intensify exposure to the realities of life. One sees more sickness and more suffering, more death, more instances of humanity's inhumanity. Reinhold Niebuhr's classic work, *Moral Man and Immoral Society*, argued quite persuasively that persons who ordinarily behave very morally as individuals are often moved to act immorally as members of a collective. It's almost as if we humans tend to lose our moral bearings when we congregate and engage in "groupthink."

Second, the Axial centers were generally characterized by political and legal upheaval. The Chinese Axial Age overlapped an epoch in Chinese history known as the Period of Warring States. In China, the traditional—and relatively stable—feudal system was disintegrating and small principalities began to vie for hegemony. The result was an extremely brutal era in which hundreds of thousands of Chinese lost their lives. The Indian ascetical movement was set in the context of profound and rapid political and economic transformation in the area surrounding the Ganges River. The Axial Age in the land of Judah proceeded under the constant threat (and eventual actuality) of the tiny nation's engulfment by the surrounding larger empires. And Zoroaster's reform of Iranian religion was undertaken at a time of great lawlessness in West Asia, as his society was plagued by independent warlords and bands of warriors with little respect for human life. Rapid political and social change, of course, generates great uncertainty and insecurity for many. But interestingly—and this is much less frequently observed—such times are often the most creative and innovative for religious and philosophical thought. The context of political and social instability fosters just the right conditions to evoke the best (as well as the worst) in human beings. With their worlds in a time of change, and their received traditions under question, the bold individuals of the Axial Age experienced a freedom to think and live their lives in new ways.

Third, sages in all the Axial centers became increasingly anxious about death and preoccupied with what, if anything, lay beyond death. Pre-Axial humans, of course, were not unconcerned with death, but they seemed more generally to accept death as a natural part of life and rarely gave attention to the idea of an afterlife. For the most part, they valued a long life with many descendents but hardly expected anything more than that. The human sense of identity prior to the Axial Age was more firmly rooted in one's participation in the family, or the clan, or the tribe. Ideas about who and what one was and what life was about were derived from being part of a larger human reality. Accordingly, death could be accepted, knowing that the family would survive one's personal demise.

But by the Axial Age, attitudes towards death began to reflect a greater concern about the experience of dying and what occurs after it. Increasingly, death was regarded with dread and fear, and speculation about what might lie beyond was filled with both hope and terror. Every conceivable possibility for the afterlife seems to have been entertained: from continued existence in a delightful place; to life in the most unpleasant realms of the underworld; to rebirth in this life; or to the decomposition of the body and soul back to the elements of the earth; or to the resurrection of the dead at the end of the age. The issues and proposals were passionately debated, an indication that something of great importance was at stake, something that marked an important change from the pre-Axial Age.

What is reflected in this shift in attitudes about death is the rise of the sense of individuality and selfhood. The Axial Age was the time when people more and more began to experience themselves as separate, autonomous individuals, as what we call *selves*. With this new sense of selfhood comes a greater consciousness of being a human being as a moral agent, accountable and responsible for his or her actions. It may seem rather odd for us modern people to hear such a thing, because we take individuality, and moral agency, and personal responsibility as givens in life, but the fact is the self—in the sense that I've just described it—comes into human existence at a particular point in time, and that was the Axial Age. Humans have not always been selves.

As human beings began to think of themselves as separate, autonomous individuals, death becomes more dreadful as a reality. Selfhood promotes a feeling of isolation—or at least differentiation—from the rest of the human community and the rest of reality, making it difficult to accept dying as part of the natural process of living in which one views oneself as merely a passing element in a greater reality. Now death means the end of the thing we hold most dear: our selves. Knowing that the world, or our descendents, or even our accomplishments, live on after us is hardly any consolation. Woody Allen even spoke in the spirit of this attitude when he said: "I don't want to achieve immortality through my work... I want to achieve it through not dying." The self does not wish to die, and it looks for ways to avoid death or at least to survive it.

Fourth, the growing sense of selfhood and anxiety about life's transience stimulated conjectures about the nature of the person and spurred the search to discover something within the human individual that might endure the dissolution of the body, something eternal or immortal. As part of this quest, Axial sages developed a new way of thinking about the world and the place of humanity within it. S. N. Eisenstadt, one of the first scholars to study the sociological dimensions of the Axial Age, calls this way of looking at life "transcendental consciousness," the ability to step back and to see the world more comprehensively—as a totality—and to look more critically and more reflectively, not merely accepting the world as it appeared or as tradition said it was.

Transcendental consciousness produced novel conceptions of the world's ultimate reality. In some cases, the Axial sages were not content to accept the old anthropomorphic gods and goddesses as the highest realities or powers governing the universe. They often conceived ultimate reality in terms transcending the ancient gods of the older religions. They imagined sublime conceptions of ultimate reality, such as the Hindu notion of Brahman and the Chinese Dao, so great that they exceeded the human capacity to think or to speak about them. And thinking about these highest or deepest realities led individuals to reflect more consciously on the process of thinking itself. Axial sages became progressively more interested in what we call epistemology, how we know what we know and what the limitations of our knowledge are. Attention to epistemology, accordingly, promoted a greater sense of self-consciousness and the awareness of humanity's place in the universe.

Finally, the Axial Age marks a dramatic change in the very function of religion in human life. During this era, the very purpose of religion shifted from what theologian John Hick calls cosmic maintenance to personal transformation. By cosmic maintenance, we mean that religion functions chiefly as a ritual means for human beings to collaborate with the divine powers to assist in keeping the world in good working order. The gods and goddesses relied on humans to help them provide the means to ensure reproduction and the productivity of the land, to keep the sun on its course, and the seasons following one after the other. Humans believed that they had to provide sacrificial food and other pleasantries to the divinities to enable and to encourage the gods to promote the processes of life. Both divine and human beings worked together to maintain the well-being of the world on which they both depended. (To understand this view of religion, you may have to set aside for a moment the belief that the gods are omnipotent and completely self-sufficient: the gods and goddesses certainly surpass humans in power and dignity at this time, but were not supreme entities that we may be accustomed to thinking of in this day and age.)

During the Axial period, however, religion takes on an unprecedented new role in human life: providing the means for the individual human being to undergo whatever change is necessary to achieve immortality or happiness or whatever the religion considered to be the highest good in life. This new function for religion comes as a consequence of the developments that we've just discussed. Selfhood and the heightened awareness of suffering and death prompted some religions to imagine a wonderful afterlife as a way of experiencing some measure of overcoming the painful realities of this life.

The achievements of these goals were connected to transforming the self from its ordinary state to some other. It might mean accepting a new vision of the way the world works, or accepting the demands of a particular god with the power to bestow immortality or paradise, or in subjecting the self to a discipline that reshapes it in more wholesome ways. However it is imagined, the rise of the self in the Axial Age means that religions have a new problematic on their hands. Religions responded to this problematic by helping people understand the nature and cause of their problems and by providing ways—innovative ways—to solve them.

I hope these few remarks have been sufficient to help you see what a significant and influential time the Axial Age was. Jaspers was certainly correct in his contention that this era laid contemporary humanity's spiritual foundations. In this series of lectures, we will probe this idea in much greater detail by carefully examining the specific and distinctive developments within the Axial centers. The focus of our attention will be the Axial centers in West, South, and East Asia, and we will discuss each sequentially. Due in part to constraints of time, we will not cover the developments in ancient Greece, except by way of comparison, or in Judah, except to discuss the impact of outside influences. Besides time restrictions, I'm omitting these areas because other courses offered by The Teaching Company have covered them far better than I could do. So if you are interested in these Axial centers, I urge you to consider the fine courses in Greek philosophy and Judaism offered by other professors through The Teaching Company.

The approach of this course is unlike that of many courses in comparative or world religions. Let me conclude with a few words about the nature of this approach and what distinguishes it from other ways of treating world religions.

If you have ever taken a course in the academic study of religion, it's likely that you have approached the subject in one of two or three basic ways. You may have taken a course on a particular tradition, such as Islam or Buddhism or Christianity. And if so, you may have studied that religion in a chronological fashion, starting from its founding (or shortly before) and proceeding historically to the present. The benefit of that general method is that it allows one to study a single religious tradition in a good deal of depth. If the approach was chronological, it added the very important dimension of showing how religions evolve over time. Without that historical perspective, one might be led to think that religious traditions are relatively static institutions or that practitioners of a particular religion believe and practice the same things. As someone whose job it is to interpret religions, I'm frequently asked questions like: What do Hindus believe? Well, the truest answer I can give to a question like that is, Hindus believe and have believed many different things throughout their history. And the same answer could be offered with regard to every major religion in the world. The danger of not taking into account historical development is neglecting this great diversity manifested in all religions. But usually in courses focused on a single tradition, comparisons with other religions are rarely made.

In the second general method of religious studies, one examines religions one-by-one, noting differences and similarities where appropriate. This is the way many world religions textbooks are structured. In the first two weeks of the course, for example, you study Hinduism, and then two weeks for Buddhism, two days on Jainism, a day on the Sikhs, three weeks on Chinese religions, and so forth. The benefit of this method is getting to study the traditions side-by-side, which helps to see how they differ and compare. It is a very difficult thing truly to understand any religion—including one's own—without comparisons with difference. In some respects, the process is like learning a new language. I never really learned English until I had to study German.

But the problem with this comparative approach is that such short period of times are spent on each religion that the treatment is often very shallow and historical development is glossed over or insufficiently discussed. Furthermore, the short time allotted to each tradition often means that the religion's development within the larger context of its culture is neglected. Thus, one fails to see how traditions are related to one another, and to their social setting, and other aspects of culture, such as art, economics, politics, and education.

This two-weeks-per-religion approach can also neglect the way religious traditions frequently influence and shape other traditions. Did you know that the use of the rosary, or prayer beads, originated with Christianity but has been since been adopted by Hindus, Buddhists, and Muslims? Or that karma and rebirth are ideas shared by Jains, Hindus, Sikhs, and Buddhists, but that they all understand them in very different terms? Or that the Roman Catholic Church canonized a Saint Josaphat, who was a fictionalized character based on the life of the Buddha? Or that some Buddhists worship Hindu gods, and that the Buddha himself is considered part of the Hindu pantheon? These are just a few quick and simple instances of the greater phenomenon of cross-fertilization between religions. Religions also develop in reaction or opposition to each other, just as Daoism emerged in part to balance the perceived excesses of Confucianism.

By examining these religions over the 600-year span of the Axial Age and against the background of their pre-Axial settings, we have the opportunity to study religions both in their historical development and comparatively. And the benefits of this approach are many. The comparative dimension allows us to view how different religions respond to similar historical and sociological circumstances, such as the urbanization and political upheavals that I mentioned earlier. It also allows us to see the mutual interactions of religions in close proximity to one another. Limiting the time frame and the number of religions that we discuss also allows us to gain a measure of depth in our investigation and connect them more fully with their social and political contexts. But the greatest value of this course, I believe, derives from the era on which it is focused. The Axial Age is simply one of the most intriguing periods in religious history. I can think of no other 600-year period that begins to compare with it in terms of the richness and creativity that it holds. We are about to observe the world's great religions coming to life.

I am very happy that you have decided to join me on this exciting tour through this astonishing and decisive moment in human history. I will do my best to make it worth your while.

Lecture Two
The Noble Ones

Scope:

Linguistic and textual analysis has conclusively shown that the people who occupied northwestern India and eastern Iran prior to the Axial Age were closely related, spoke similar languages, and held common religious beliefs. Most scholars think that these Indo-Iranians descended from the same stock of pastoral nomads who originated in the Central Asian steppes. A small minority, however, believe that these people were indigenous to India. This lecture explores the culture and religion of Indo-Iranians prior to their split into two separate groups. The Rig Veda and the Avesta, which later became the foundational scriptures of Hinduism and Zoroastrianism, respectively, give us a glimpse of the Indo-Iranians' gods, their social and moral structures, their cosmology, and their ritual practices. Essentially, their religion served to provide the means for the Indo-Iranians to attain the goods necessary for a prosperous and stable life on Earth. The gods were entreated to help maintain productivity and harmony in the here-and-now rather than to secure otherworldly salvation.

Outline

I. To understand the changes in the Axial centers of East, West, and South Asia, we begin in Central Asia a millennium before the Axial Age, examining the cultural and religious practices of people living in the south Russian steppes, what is today roughly Ukraine to West Kazakhstan. Most scholars believe that these pre-Axial peoples gradually migrated to northern Europe, the northern Mediterranean region, Iran, India, and as far west as Ireland.

A. The Indo-Iranians remained together until about 4,000 years ago, when they split, some venturing into present-day Iraq and others to present-day Afghanistan and the Indus Valley, gradually spreading across northern India.

B. For this lecture, we are most interested in the period when the two groups were united in Central Asia before heading south into what is now Iran and India. We call these people the *Indo-Iranians*.

C. As the descendants of the Indo-Europeans scattered throughout Eurasia, their single language evolved into dozens of languages in the Indo-European family. Analysis of Icelandic, German, Gaelic, Latin, Greek, Russian, Persian, Sanskrit, Sinhalese, and English shows evidence that they all derived from a single language.

D. As the group divided, their languages evolved separately but were still similar enough to enable communication. The Indian tribes spoke a form of Sanskrit, and the Iranian tribes spoke Avestan, which now exists only in a collection of sacred writings called the Avesta.

E. The Indo-Iranians referred to themselves as the "Noble Ones," each arriving at their respective destinations, which they called the "Land of the Noble."

II. What we know of Indo-Iranian culture comes from two sources preserved in oral tradition: the Rig Veda, the oldest extant Indo-European text, and the Avesta, a slightly later text from Iran.

A. The Indo-Iranians were nomadic and semi-nomadic animal herders who also hunted wild animals.

B. Tribes had little to no formal governance. The society was divided into priests and "producers," that is, essentially everyone who was not a priest.

C. The Indo-Iranians were likely peaceful people, with a static society that, for centuries, experienced few significant cultural changes.

D. Having not yet tamed horses, the earliest people didn't travel far and knew nothing of warfare that horses made possible.

III. The religious life of early Indo-Iranians suggests a commonsensical worldview with a belief in numerous gods. Trees were also venerated, especially those growing along riverbanks, probably because the bark or fruit was thought to have healing properties.

A. The various gods related to different aspects of everyday life, but especially important were those who controlled the natural world: Sky and Earth (Asman and Zam), Sun and

Moon (Hvar and Mah), and winds (Vata and Vayu).

B. The Indo-Iranians worshiped an overarching "king of the gods," who eventually became irrelevant and was forgotten. The Iranians called him Dyaoš, and the Indians called him Dyaus-Pitr, later known as the Greek and Roman gods Zeus and Jupiter.

C. Gods associated with ritual practices were also important and included the gods of fire, water, animal spirits, and a vision-inducing substance called *haoma* in the Avestan dialect and *soma* in Sanskrit.

D. The *ahuras* (Avestan) or *asuras* (Sanskrit) were gods simply called "lords." Three were of greatest significance.

1. The first two were associated with oaths, which humans had little means to enforce; therefore, gods were invoked to punish those who failed their oaths.

2. The third and greatest of the *ahuras* was Mazda, the Lord of Wisdom, who was, later in the Iranian tradition, represented by the Sun.

E. There were numerous lesser divinities called the "shiny ones,"—*devas* (Sanskrit) or *daevas* (Avestan)—who represented courage, friendship, justice, obedience, and glory, also called charisma.

IV. In addition to a complex world of spirits and gods, the Indo-Iranians believed in an abstract principle of cosmic order, which kept the Sun on its path and the seasons in proper sequence. Obedience to moral law promoted harmony and well-being, and rituals played an important role in maintaining this order.

A. *Rta* (Sanskrit) or *asha* (Avestan) represented an absolute principle for appropriate human and divine behavior; deities were also subject to *rta*/*asha*.

B. The principle of order was opposed by the power of disharmony and chaos, called *druj* (Avestan) or *druh* (Sanskrit).

C. Rituals were needed to maintain *rta*/*asha* against the diametrically opposed *druj*/*druh*. In this, we see an example of the pre-Axial practice of cosmic maintenance based on the responsibility people felt to influence the processes on which their lives depended.

D. To fully understand how these ritual practices promoted social and cosmological harmony, we need to look at the Indo-Iranians' creation stories. The Avestan version says that the Earth was created in seven stages.

1. First, the sky was conceived as a gigantic inverted bowl made of beautiful stone. Second, water was created, covering the bottom of the sky shell. Third, solid earth was created, floating on the water.
2. In the fourth, fifth, and sixth stages, life was added in the form of one plant, one animal—a bull—and one man, named Yima (Avestan) or Yama (Sanskrit). In the seventh stage, fire was added.
3. In the final act of creation, the gods performed the first ritual sacrifice. By crushing and dismembering the plant, the bull, and the man, they created new life. The world was now populated and began the course of *asha* through death and reproduction.

E. From simple to complex rituals, the Indo-Iranians reenacted the gods' primordial sacrifices to maintain cosmic and moral order and to ensure that new life replaced the old.

1. Among the simplest rituals were offerings to the gods of water and fire. Milk and two plant leaves, to represent the animal and vegetable realms, were offered to water. Incense, wood, and animal fat were offered to fire.
2. A sacred space was created for more complex rituals, in which priests uttered prayers to keep out evil spirits while fires burned in sacred vessels.
3. Fire rituals were the most sacred, often involving the blood of goats, sheep, or cattle. Animal sacrifices were performed with special prayers so that the animal's spirit could continue as part of a divine being called the *Soul of the Bull*, the life energy of animals.
4. Consecrated and cooked meat was offered to other gods and then eaten. The Indo-Iranians ate only consecrated meat from domesticated animals. They also said prayers before killing wild animals to ensure their spirits' safe return to the Soul of the Bull.

5. Some rituals involved a sacred beverage, *soma* (Sanskrit) or *haoma* (Avestan). *Soma* was believed to be a god that lived in a plant whose properties induced ecstasy, a sense of immortality, freedom from suffering and fear, and communion with the spirit world. The experience of divine communion was important in confirming the existence of the gods while expanding the mind to consider the deepest possibilities of human life.

V. We now arrive at the eve of the Axial Age, although further developments in Indo-Iranian religions will occur first. The central purpose of religion at this time was co-creation with the gods in the processes and functions of life. Forces were often personified as gods or goddesses or as abstract, impersonal principles. Human beings, clearly feeling a kinship with the natural and divine worlds, had to keep their world in good working order.

Essential Reading:

Boyce, *Zoroastrians*, chapter 1.

Supplementary Reading:

Foltz, *Spirituality in the Land of the Noble*, chapter 1.

O'Flaherty, *The Rig-Veda*, "Soma."

Questions to Consider:

1. The Indo-Iranians believed that the gods themselves were subject to *rta*/*asha*, the principle of order and morality. Many theologians have objected to such a view because it implies a reality above god. The issue of the divine's relationship to morality led Socrates to ask in the *Euthyphro*: "Are morally good acts willed by God because they are morally good, or are they morally good because they are willed by God?" What do you think? Does the matter turn on how the divine is conceived?
2. Do you think the value of spiritual experiences is invalidated if they are induced by physical substances, such as *soma*/*haoma*?

Lecture Two—Transcript
The Noble Ones

Our story begins neither in East, West, or South Asia, nor in the Axial Age. To understand the great changes in these Axial centers, we must begin in Central Asia at least a millennium before the Axial Age gets underway. We will be looking at the culture and religious practices of people living in the area of the south Russian steppes, east of the Volga River and north of the Caspian Sea. Today, this region roughly corresponds to the land from Ukraine to West Kazakhstan. Five thousand years ago, this area was mostly barren desert that saw little rainfall and suffered bitterly cold winters and harsh summers. It was not an easy place in which to live.

We don't know a great deal about the inhabitants of the Central Asian steppes in the pre-Axial period. But one thing most scholars believe is that many of the original occupants of this area and their descendants gradually migrated to other parts of the world, including northern Europe, the northern Mediterranean region, as far west as Ireland, and southward into Iran and India. Through careful analysis of languages as diverse as Icelandic, German, Gaelic, Latin and Greek, Russian, Persian, Sanskrit, Sinhalese, and, of course, English, the modern discipline of linguistics has determined that these languages derive from what was once a single language. Linguists have tried to reconstruct that original language, but it has proven to be an elusive task. Over time, as the descendants of these Central Asians scattered throughout Eurasia, this single language evolved into the dozens of languages and dialects that we refer to as the Indo-European family of languages.

Of the many groups that migrated from this region to other locations, the one we're most interested in are those who migrated southward, into the regions now occupied by the countries of Iran and India. To differentiate this group from the other members of the Indo-European peoples, we'll refer to them as the Indo-Iranians. This group remained together until about 4,000 years ago when it too slowly split and moved in two separate directions. You won't need a Ph.D. to figure out that the Iranian branch went into the land of Iran. Some of them ventured further into Mesopotamia, the area of present-day Iraq; the Indo branch went into Afghanistan and then into the Indus Valley, gradually spreading across northern India. As Indo-Iranians divided, their languages evolved from one another, but they were similar enough that communication was still possible. The Iranian tribes spoke a dialect we call Avestan, because now it only exists in a collection of sacred writings known as the Avesta. The group that migrated to India spoke a form of the language we now know as Sanskrit.

Of course, these people did not refer to themselves as Indo-Iranians. They called themselves *ariya*, a term that translates into English as noble. So their self-designation was the noble ones. When each group arrived at its final destination they called their new territory the land of the noble. The Indian group knew their new home not as India but as *Aryavarta*, and the Iranians called theirs *Airyana vaejah*, the name that eventually evolved into the term Iran. The name Ireland, by the way, has a similar derivation and also means the land of the noble. To keep matters straight, we'll use the term Indo-Aryans to refer to the group that settled in India and the word Iranians to designate the group that ended up in Iran, that is, after they split.

The principal focus of our discussion for this lecture is not on these groups *after* their separation but on the time when they were united in Central Asia and beginning their southward movement. For this period, we'll simply call them the Indo-Iranians. In subsequent talks, we'll have the opportunity to dwell on these groups separately and compare and contrast them.

Basically, what we know of the Indo-Iranians comes from two sources: the Rig Veda, the oldest extant Indo-European text, and the Avesta, a slightly later text from Iran that was preserved in oral tradition, just as the Rig Veda was. Because they were composed before the split, the Rig Veda and the Avesta tell us a good bit about Indo-Iranian life. I'll talk more about these texts, their composition, and their role in the construction of religion in ancient India and Iran in later talks. For now, we're interested in what they tell us about the common Indo-Iranian life.

The Rig Veda and Avesta make clear that these peoples were nomadic and semi-nomadic shepherds and cattle herders, who wandered around in relatively small areas seeking pastureland for their animals. Since the steppes were rather arid and barren, the Indo-Iranians were not great agriculturalists. The principal source of their food, therefore, was the domesticated animals that they kept and the wild animals they hunted.

Their society was essentially divided into priests and everyone else, who were called the producers because of their work. They arranged themselves into tribes with little to no formal governing structures. Early Indo-Iranian society appears to have been relatively peaceful and probably rather static. It seems to have existed for centuries with little significant cultural changes. Since they had not yet tamed the horse, the earliest Indo-Iranians did not travel very far and they knew nothing of the kind of warfare that the horse made possible for other societies.

The early religious life of the Indo-Iranians, as much as it can be reconstructed from our limited resources, suggests a rather commonsensical view for people living in the harsh environment of Central Asia. Like almost all ancient groups, the Indo-Iranians had their gods, their beliefs about the nature of the world, and their rituals that helped them understand and influence those gods and that world.

The gods were of various sorts, related to different aspects of everyday life. Especially important to the ordinary people were the gods who controlled the parts of the natural world. These gods included the Sky and the Earth—known as Asman and Zam—the Sun and the Moon—Hvar and Mah, as they were called—and the winds—Vata and Vayu. And although not considered gods, as such, trees were especially venerated, especially those growing beside rivers or streams, probably because the bark or fruit was thought to have healing properties. Still, today in India certain trees growing by rivers are seen as highly auspicious and often mark the place of a temple or a sacred shrine. At one time the Indo-Iranians worshiped an overarching sky god—a kind of king of the gods—but over time, he became so remote and distant from everyday life that he simply became irrelevant and the Aryans effectively forgot about him. In the Iranian dialect he was called Dyaoš and in the Indian dialect he was known as Dyaus-Pitr. Both names are cognates of the Greek and Roman terms for their chief sky gods, Zeus and Jupiter.

In addition to the gods of nature, the gods associated with ritual practices were particularly important, namely, the Fire, the Water, a deity called the Soul of the Bull, and a vision-inducing substance called *haoma* in the Avestan dialect and *soma* in the Sanskrit. These divinities were especially significant to the priests, and I'll have more to say about them in a moment, when we discuss ritual.

A third category of divine beings was the *ahuras* in Avestan, or *asuras* in Sanskrit, words that simply mean lord. In this class of gods, three were of greatest significance. The first two were associated with oaths and promise keeping. Making oaths and pledges, of course, are important in any society, but not all cultures in the ancient world had the human means to enforce such covenants and agreements. It was not uncommon, therefore, for the gods to be invoked to punish individuals who failed to live up to their oaths. We still have a vestige of this practice in certain legal proceedings where an individual swears to do something, like tell the truth, and then concludes, "So help me, god." The ancients might have added an additional clause, something like "and may I be smitten by god so-and-so if I fail to honor my word."

Among the Indo-Iranians, pledges and oaths were originally believed to carry a divine power in themselves, sufficient to enforce the promise. Over time this power resident in the words became personified and associated with two anthropomorphic deities who took their names from the two kinds of promises that one could make. Their names were Varuna and Mithra.

The third and greatest of the *ahuras*, however, was Mazda, the Lord of Wisdom. That is Mazda, spelled just like the name of the car. The car, by the way, was so named for three reasons: first, to honor the god Mazda; and second, because Mazda still means in Persian, wisdom; and third, because the family name of the Japanese manufacturer is Matsuda, which when Anglicized sounds a lot like Mazda. But in the ancient world, Mazda was not originally associated with vehicles or any physical phenomenon. However, later in the Iranian tradition, he is represented by the sun. When we take up the Zoroastrian reform of this ancient tradition in the next lecture, we'll see how Lord Mazda assumes a very prominent role, becoming the most important god of all for the Iranians.

And finally, there were numerous lesser divinities called the shiny ones. In Sanskrit, shiny one translates the word *deva* and in Avestan the word *daeva*. Both words have obvious cognates in other Indo-European languages. You can think of *deus* in Latin or divine in English. The shiny ones represented such qualities as courage, friendship, justice, obedience, and glory—a quality that dwells in gods and heroes and prophets, like charisma we might say today. In the later Indo-Aryan tradition, *deva* (and its female form, *devi*) are terms for the most important class of divinities, although that was not the case in Iran.

In addition to this rather complex world of spirits and gods, the Indo-Iranians believed in a more abstract, impersonal principle of order. The Sanskrit speakers called it *rta*, and the Avestan speakers referred to it as *asha*. Both words designate a kind of natural law that maintained cosmic order, keeping the sun on its path and the seasons following in proper sequence. *Rta* and *asha* had moral as well as cosmological dimensions, and in this sense represented an absolute principle for appropriate human behavior—and, I might add, divine behavior since the deities themselves were also subject to *rta*/*asha*.

Obedience of the moral law promoted harmony and well being for the individual and for society, but the principle of order was also opposed by another power that accounted for disharmony and chaos. The Iranians, for whom this element of disorder became very prominent in later theology, called it *druj*. Because these two principles were diametrically opposed to one another, kind of in a constant struggle for dominance, the Indo-Iranians considered it necessary to help maintain and strengthen asha, the orderly element. They believed they could do so by ritual means. Proper observance of the religious rites thus enhanced the power of asha and promoted harmony in the world. Now, this is one instance of the pre-Axial practice of cosmic maintenance, based on the responsibility that people felt for collaborating with the processes on which their lives depended.

So let's turn now to these ritual practices and observe the ways they promoted social and cosmological harmony. To fully understand pre-Axial rituals in any culture, it's important that we have a good grasp of its beliefs about the origins of the world, those things that are found in its cosmogonies, or creation stories. Cosmogonies generally provided prototypes or templates for ritual practices. The performers of religious rites often understood themselves as reenacting the divine work of creation, and thereby renewing creation and giving it a fresh beginning.

To illustrate this point, I'll start with a brief retelling of the world's creation taken from the Avestan texts and then show its relationship to ritual practices. The Rig Veda also has its cosmogonies—actually, quite a few of them—and we'll deal with those in due time.

The Avestan version says that the Earth was created in seven stages, not unlike the seven-day scheme that we find in the book of Genesis, which was actually written centuries later. The driving force behind the Avestan creation story—whether a god or gods—isn't really clear, although sometimes it appears to be the work of the Ahura Mazda.

In the first stage, the sky came into being. Now, the sky was conceived to be something like a gigantic inverted bowl made of beautiful stone. Now, to me, thinking of the sky as a solid hemisphere is just profoundly sensible. Rather than believing that the sky was our perception of infinite space, as we moderns might think, it seemed obvious to the ancients that it was a finite, solid structure. I remember as a kid thinking the very same thing when I pondered the nature of the sky. When the first manned rockets were being sent into space, I recall being deeply worried about the possibility of spacecraft possibly literally shattering the sky and breaking it into pieces.

In the second stage of creation, water was created, covering the bottom of the sky shell. Imagine an upside down bowl floating on the surface of the water in your kitchen sink, and you have a general model for this worldview. Now let a salad plate also float on the water's surface underneath the sky-bowl, and you've added the third stage: the creation of the solid earth, like a flat dish afloat on water.

In the fourth, fifth, and sixth stages, life was added to the physical world. Originally, there was one plant, then one animal—a bull—and finally a man, named Yima in Avestan and Yama in Sanskrit. And in the seventh stage, fire was added, an element pervading the entire created world, residing in seen and unseen places.

In the final act of creation, the gods assembled to perform the first ritual act, a sacrifice. By crushing and dismembering the primordial plant, the bull, and the man, the gods created new lives, and the vegetable, animal, and human realms were populated and the world set in motion following the course of asha. Death soon appeared, as did reproduction and new life, and the world was on its way.

In a ritual setting, the Indo-Iranians reenacted this primordial sacrifice to maintain the cosmic and moral order and to ensure that new life properly replaced the old. The rituals they performed were of many sorts, from the simple to the complex.

Among the simplest were offerings of libations to the gods of Water and of Fire. In the arid and cold steppes region the very importance of—indeed, the very sacredness of—these two elements is readily evident. To Water was given a libation of milk and two plant leaves to represent the animal and vegetable realms. These libations returned to the divine powers the vital elements that they required to continue productivity and harmony. The Water goddess was strengthened by these gifts.

Fire was of great importance not only for winter warmth but also for cooking meat, the staple of the Indo-Iranian diet. Because starting a fire was difficult, fires were kept continually burning in the fireplaces and terracotta pots. Like libations to Water, offerings to Fire were from the two kingdoms: incense and wood from plants and animal fat from cooked meat. The melting fat made the flames to blaze up, visibly fortifying the fire.

For more complex rituals, a sacred space had to be created and professional priests were required to conduct them. Because of their nomadic life, the ritual precinct was temporary and portable. Sacred space was marked by lines drawn on the ground as prayers were uttered to keep out evil spirits. Fires burned in sacred vessels and in pits dug in the ground.

The most sacred of these fire rituals often involved blood sacrifice, usually goats, sheep, or cattle. The Avestan word for sacrifice was *yasna*, almost identical to the Sanskrit term *yajña*. The Indo-Iranians were awed by the act of taking life and they did so reverentially. Animal sacrifices had to be performed with special prayers to enable the animal's spirit or life force to continue on. Obviously, this suggests a strong affinity between humans and animals. One of the Avestan texts even says "We reverence our own souls, and those of domestic animals which nourish us…and the souls of useful wild animals." The spirits of sacrificed animals were believed to become a part of the divine being called the Soul of the Bull, the life energy of the animal world. Animal blood actually nourished this deity, and in so doing, the Indo-Iranians were helping the god to care for the animals on earth and to guarantee their abundance.

Consecrated and cooked meat was also offered to the other gods and then eaten by the participants of the sacrifice. Because of their respect for animal life, the Indo-Iranians only ate consecrated meat from their domesticated animals. Even before killing a wild animal for food, hunters said prayers to ensure the animal spirit's safe return to the Soul of the Bull.

The priests led rituals that also involved another element, a beverage known by *soma* in Sanskrit or *haoma* in Avestan. This substance, like Fire and Water, was regarded as a god and resided in a special species of plant whose identity is unknown to us today and maybe was even unknown to the Indo-Iranians after their departure from Central Asia. The liquid essence of these plants was pressed out and then mixed as a golden drink resembling honey.

Soma had properties that allowed those who imbibed it to feel ecstatic, literally out of their ordinary world and transported to the realm of the gods. This passage from the Rig Veda captures a sense of the experience of consuming *soma*:

We Have Drunk the *Soma*

> I have tasted the sweet drink of life, knowing that it inspires good thoughts and joyous expansiveness to the extreme, that all the gods and mortals seek it together, calling it… [ambrosia].
>
> When you penetrate inside, you will know no limits, and you will avert the wrath of the gods. …
>
> We have drunk the *soma*; we have become immortal; we have gone to the light; we have found the gods. What can hatred and the malice of a mortal do to us now, O immortal one? …
>
> The glorious drops that I have drunk set me free in wide space…. Let the drops protect me from the foot that stumbles and keep lameness away from me.
>
> Inflame me like a fire kindled by friction; make us see far; make us richer, better. I am intoxicated with you, *soma*, I think myself rich. Draw near and make us thrive. …

> Weakness and diseases have gone; the forces of darkness have fled in terror. *Soma* has climbed in us, expanding. We have come to the place where they stretch out life spans.

By ingesting *soma*, the Indo-Iranians achieved what they considered to be the apex of existence: the sense of immortality; freedom from suffering and fear; communion with the gods and the spirit world; and intense pleasure. Little wonder that *soma* was so highly prized and zealously protected. Its chief downside, however, was that it provided only temporary ecstasy. Eventually the effects would wear off, and ordinary life would reassert itself. But the experience of divine communion was important in confirming the existence of the gods and expanding the mind to consider the deepest possibilities of human life. *Soma* allowed the Indo-Iranians to imagine a life free of suffering and fear. In the centuries to come, the heirs of these traditions would seek similar experiences through the techniques of introspection and ascetic practice rather than physical substances.

We have now come to that point in history on the eve of the Axial Age, although further developments in Indo-Iranian religions will occur before it dawns. But we are at a place where we can make some solid statements about Indo-Iranian religion that will enable us to understand the axial transformation that will occur in Iran and India later. We have observed that the central purpose of religion at this time, for these peoples, was essentially to collaborate in the processes and functions of life. These forces were often personified as gods and goddesses, or as an abstract, impersonal principle. Human beings had to do their part to keep both the natural world and the social world in good working order, and it was clear that they felt a close kinship with other aspects of the natural and divine worlds.

In our next talk, we will return to see some fundamental changes to this picture of Indo-Iranian religious life, and we'll see the final split between the Indo-Aryans and the Iranians. Then we'll investigate the changes that occurred in Iran and the consequences of those changes for the religions of Semitic origin. After that, we'll see what happens when the Aryans get to India.

Lecture Three
The World of Zoroaster

Scope:

The Avesta suggests that the culture of the Indo-Iranians had degenerated into widespread lawlessness some time before the Axial period. In response to the anarchy of these times, Zoroaster, one of the most mysterious individuals among the founders of Axial religions, arose to reform and purify the ancient religion that he served as priest. We know very little about the man himself, and there is considerable debate about when he even lived. Some scholars place him a few centuries before the start of the Axial Age, but there may be good reasons for including him in the lineup of Axial sages, not the least of which is his deep concern with morality and the ultimate destiny of the individual. Zoroaster's ethical sensitivities led him to reinterpret the deities of the Iranian pantheon, effectively making them partisans of either good or evil. His reforms eventually led to a new religious tradition bearing his name.

Outline

I. The Indo-Iranians viewed cultural or religious innovation with suspicion and regarded change as sacrilegious. However, as they drifted south from Central Asia, they came in contact with the Mesopotamians, and their way of life changed dramatically.

- **A.** From the Mesopotamians, the Indo-Iranians learned how to domesticate horses, build war chariots, and fashion weapons, completely disrupting their once stable culture.
- **B.** They turned to stealing livestock, and raiding and pillaging brought with it a fundamental new purpose: to gain wealth and glory.
- **C.** But this lifestyle disrupted moral concerns and respect for the rule of law. Perpetrators showed little regard for the weak and defenseless.
- **D.** With this new way of life arose a third class of individuals alongside the priests and producers: the warlords and professional warriors.

II. Society now had both peaceful people and warriors, and new nomenclature entered the vocabulary to distinguish between the two.

- **A.** In ancient Iran, the *ashavans* followed the way of order and stability. Followers of *asha* were thought to be blessed, suggesting divine approval.
- **B.** The wicked ones were the *drujvants*, devotees of the principle of disorder. Many worshiped Indra, the brave new deity of the heroic age.
- **C.** New gods more acceptable to the emerging warrior caste began to appear and even dominate some forms of religion.
  - **1.** Indra was valiant in combat, reckless, and amoral but loyal to those who revered him and made offerings to him. In return, he was a giver of many gifts to his followers.
  - **2.** Indra loved *soma*, the intoxicating drink that fueled his passion and reckless spirit.
    - **a.** In earlier times, Indo-Iranians used *soma* to commune with the gods, to feel immortal, and to imagine a new life free of distress.
    - **b.** In the heroic age of raiding, *soma* acquired another dimension, freeing its potential to produce a frenzy conducive to war and lawlessness.
- **D.** In contrast to Indra, other gods, such as Varuna, began to fall by the wayside in ritual and celebration. The adventurous life of the daring Indra was more appealing, and in time, Varuna and Indra would come to be seen as diametrically opposite gods.

III. By the middle of the second millennium B.C.E., the Indo-Iranian peoples were gradually diverging to their respective lands. Our story now follows the peoples of Iran, among whom emerged Zoroaster (a Greek transliteration of *Zarathustra*), who is one of the least-known founding figures in the history of the world's religions, a transitional figure, representing an interesting mixture of pre-Axial and Axial religious elements.

- **A.** Little is known about Zoroaster, including when and where he lived. Roughly, we date him to around 1200 B.C.E. in the eastern area of present-day Iran. He came from a modest family living in the semi-nomadic conditions of the Indo-Iranian period when cattle rustlers and outlaws were in their prime.

B. A text called the Gathas ("verses"), part of the oldest Avesta, is the foundational scripture of Zoroaster's religion and may have been composed by Zoroaster himself. More spontaneous prayers addressed to a god, as opposed to sermons or didactic proclamations, the Gathas are written in an archaic dialect close to the Sanskrit of the Rig Veda.

C. The Gathas tell us that Zoroaster was a priest, an authorized ritual specialist.

D. Troubled by the violence and lawlessness of the land, Zoroaster sought deeper truths. At age 30, he had an impressive visionary experience in which he was led into the presence of the Ahura Mazda and six other radiant beings, known collectively as the *heptad* (the "seven"), from whom he received a special revelation.

E. He now had a purpose: "[to] …teach men to seek the right [*asha*]." Though he continued to have revelations, this was clearly the turning point in his life, transforming him from priest to prophet, a critic of religious practices and a mouthpiece for a god.

IV. Zoroaster's response to his new vocation was both conservative and revolutionary. He called his fellow Iranians to return to the principles of good, order, and harmony. But he added novel dimensions to create a powerful vision of the world. There were two chief thrusts of Zoroaster's theology, both movements in the direction of simplification.

A. First, Zoroaster wanted the Ahura Mazda to be seen as superior to Varuna and the other *ahuras*, and he became a passionate advocate for worshiping Mazda as the foremost deity.

1. In his vision of the *heptad*, Zoroaster saw Mazda as the dominant deity. In later reflections, Zoroaster suggested that all the other *ahuras* and divinities were actually emanations or partial manifestations of Mazda.

2. Zoroaster believed Mazda to be the only uncreated god, who himself created the world in seven stages. This view tended toward monotheism and probably contributed to the religious environment that would ultimately champion this idea.

B. Second, Zoroaster assigned clear moral qualities to the gods. All the spirits—the *daevas* and the *ahuras*—were now plainly either good or evil.

1. Because the *daevas*, such as Indra, were honored by the cattle rustlers, Zoroaster reserved the word *daeva* exclusively for the wicked gods and the word *ahura* for the ethical gods.
2. He called the good spirits or divine assistants *yazatas*, beings associated with the principles of good and truth.
3. Zoroaster also suggested the existence of an independent evil deity, a chief god among the *daevas*, called by various names but more commonly Ahriman. Thus, two superior beings—one completely good, the other completely evil—were locked in mortal combat, each struggling for triumph.

V. In one of the ancient Gathas, Zoroaster's theological perceptions are briefly reviewed in a cryptic text called "The Two Spirits." In this short poem, he describes the two original spirits of good and evil appearing as twins. One problem with this overriding theology is that if Mazda were the original uncreated and wholly benevolent god, where did the evil spirit come from and why?

A. Zoroaster doesn't attempt to resolve the issue. What is important for him is not an abstract question of theological consistency but the pragmatic and existentially vital point that people must choose between good and evil.

B. Irrespective of the origins of these entities, humans cannot escape their responsibility in aligning themselves with good or evil and must live accordingly.

C. Thus, Zoroaster instigates the transformations of the Axial Age in his call to make a choice between good and evil, to accept personal responsibility for one's actions and words.

D. The call to this kind of personal obligation is novel in religious history because it is connected with new ideas about what it means to be human and divine.

E. Later, we'll see that for Zoroaster, an individual's moral and religious decisions determine the quality of his or her personal destiny. One's future well-being, especially in the world beyond this one, depends on one's behavior here and now. This idea was both new for the times and common in and across the Axial centers.

Essential Reading:

Boyce, *Zoroastrians*, chapters 2–3.

Supplementary Reading:

Foltz, *Spirituality in the Land of the Noble*, chapter 2.

Malandra, *An Introduction to Ancient Iranian Religion*, Introduction, chapters 1–2.

Questions to Consider:

1. What are the theological benefits and liabilities of conceiving the source of evil as within the godhead? What are the benefits and liabilities of locating the source of evil outside of god?
2. The *drujvants'* aspirations seemed to be embodied in the god Indra to a remarkable degree. Are we fated to worship gods who are merely reflections of our own beliefs and values?

Lecture Three—Transcript
The World of Zoroaster

In our last talk, we introduced a group of tribal nomads from Central Asia called the Indo-Iranians. I characterized those people as relatively peaceful and their society as relatively static. This fairly conservative culture was buttressed by religious practices focusing on cosmic maintenance, keeping the world working in an orderly fashion. Such an orientation to life is not especially interested in change. Innovation in such societies was often viewed with suspicion and frequently regarded as sacrilegious, because it represented a departure from the primordial acts of the gods. But despite these conservative forces at work in Indo-Iranian society, the way of life for these people did eventually and dramatically change. Today we'll discuss the nature of those changes and the consequences they had for religious life on the threshold of the Axial Age.

As the Indo-Iranians drifted southward from Central Asian steppes, they came in contact with one of the great civilizations of the ancient world: the Mesopotamians. Shortly after establishing this connection, the Indo-Iranians learned from the Mesopotamians how to domesticate the horse and how to build and use war chariots. They learned how to make bronze and availed themselves of the rich ore deposits of the area to fashion weapons. Their world would soon change.

The coming of the chariot and the war implements completely disrupted the once stable culture. A new form of livelihood now emerged to supplement the passive tending of sheep and cows, and that was *stealing* sheep and cows. Many of the later Indo-Iranians became what we would call cattle rustlers. Raiding and pillaging became a new way of life, initiating a restless, heroic age, not unlike the cultures of the old Norsemen and pre-Islamic Arabia. A career in raiding brought with it a fundamental new purpose to those who partook of this way of life: to gain wealth and glory. Now, cattle and sheep had long been the measure of prosperity among the Indo-Iranians. Besides providing meat and milk, these animals were the sources of leather and bones for tools, dung for fire, even urine for the consecration of the sacred implements used in the rituals.

But raiding not only altered the economy of the Indo-Iranians; it also disrupted moral concerns and respect for the rule of law. These pillaging cattle rustlers showed little regard for the weak and defenseless: whole villages might be wiped out in an afternoon just to enhance another clan's livestock holdings. Might rather than right ruled the day. With this new form of life there arose a third class of individuals alongside the priests and the producers: the warlords and professional warriors. This new class soon became identified with their love for rough living, and hard drinking, and gambling. In many ways, these images are similar to the Hollywood versions of the old American West, with its outlaws, and gunslingers, and saloons. Of course, the extent to which the Old West really was like this is a matter of debate, but I think the analogy with the Hollywood representation of the West is apt. There was an excitement and a thrill to living on the edge and outside the constraints of conventional society.

Not all the Indo-Iranians adopted the cattle rustling and village pillaging lifestyle, just as not all denizens of the Old West were cowboys and outlaws. You still had your schoolmarms and the sodbusters and the Ben and Hoss and Little Joe Cartwright-types. And actually a new kind of nomenclature enters the vocabulary to distinguish the two kinds of people. In the T.V. westerns, it was the good guys and the bad guys, the white hats and the black hats: in ancient Iran, the *ashavans* followed the way of order, the path of stability, but the wicked ones (at least so called by the *ashavans*) were the *drujvants*, the devotees of the principle of disorder.

And, just like the guys with white and black hats, the ashavans and drujvants could be imaged differently. The followers of asha were believed to have been given a heavenly blessing, which suggested divine approval. The blessing was represented as golden flames surrounding the head and it was often associated with depictions of the gods and heroes. Similar motifs can be seen in later images of the Buddha, and Christian saints, and even Muhammad, and may have indeed derived from this Iranian influence.

Even though not all Indo-Iranians were cattle rustlers and outlaws, the raiding and looting life had ramifications for those who wanted nothing to do with it. These effects were even felt in Indo-Iranian religious life. New gods more acceptable to the emerging warrior caste began to appear and even dominate some forms of religion. Many turned to worship Indra, the brave new deity of the heroic age. In fact, by the time the Rig Veda gets to India, Indra is already the ascendant divine being. Over one-quarter of the 1,000 hymns of praise are addressed to him alone.

Indra was a macho god, to be sure. He was valiant in combat, reckless to the point of being foolhardy, pretty much amoral, but loyal to those who revered him and made offerings to him. In return, he was a giver of many gifts to his followers. And he loved drinking *soma*, the intoxicating drink that fueled his passion and reckless spirit. In our previous talk, I mentioned how *soma* was imbibed to allow the Indo-Iranians to commune with the gods, to feel themselves immortal, to imagine a new life freed of distress, and to inspire poetry written by the poets. In the heroic age of raiding, *soma* seems to have acquired another dimension. Maybe it had been there all the along, but certainly in these latter days its' potential to produce a frenzy conducive to war and lawlessness was fully exploited.

Here's another passage from the Rig Veda, a little bit later than the one I read earlier. "Yes this is my thought: I will win a cow and a horse." Now, "win" here is probably a euphemism for steal.

> I will win a cow and a horse. Have I not drunk *soma*?
>
> Like impetuous winds, the drinks have lifted me up. Have I not drunk *soma*?
>
> The drinks have lifted me up, like swift horses bolting with a chariot. Have I not drunk *soma*? …
>
> The five tribes are no more to me than a mote in the eye. Have I not drunk *soma*? …
>
> In my vastness, I have surpassed the sky and this vast earth. Have I not drunk *soma*?
>
> Yes! I will place the earth here, or perhaps there. Have I not drunk *soma*? …
>
> I am huge, huge! Flying to the cloud. Have I not drunk *soma*?
>
> I am going to a well-stocked house, carrying oblations to the gods. Have I not drunk *soma*?

Where *soma* enabled the priests to see visions of the gods and poets to utter great, beautiful words, the warriors now felt themselves invincible, powerful beyond the confines of worldly limits.

In contrast to Indra, some of the other gods began to suffer decline, by which I mean, they were not given so much attention in ritual and cultic celebration. Varuna, the venerable old Ahura I mentioned last time, seemed to many to be a little too tame, sitting up in his palace in heaven keeping order in the world. For a nomadic people now equipped with the horse and chariot, the more adventurous life of the daring Indra was more appealing—or at least that's what's suggested by the texts just by the sheer volume of songs written to the various gods. In time, Varuna and Indra would come to be seen as virtually diametrically opposite gods.

Well, it is now time to let the two branches of the Indo-Iranian family part company and send them to their respective lands where we will witness the transformation of their relatively homogenous religion into the traditions that we will much later call Zoroastrianism and Hinduism. The split was gradual, of course, and the religious developments were incremental in nature. The actual divergence between the branches may have begun in the third millennium B.C.E., but it was definitely underway by the mid-second millennium. Dates—especially for nomadic peoples—are notoriously difficult to establish with precision because they leave very few archaeological artifacts.

We will first turn to West Asia, particularly the land of Iran, and then later trace the movements of the Indo-Aryans into South Asia. I want to start with Iran because the story there begins with a figure who is not exactly a full-blown Axial sage, but one whose life and thought seems to prefigure much of what is to come in the more prominent Axial centers. Zoroaster—or Zarathustra—is one of the least-known founding figures in the history of the world's religions. And we'll start with him because he is a transitional figure, representing an interesting mix of pre-axial and axial religious elements.

I suspect most of you have heard the name Zoroaster, or perhaps the name Zarathustra. Zoroaster is a later Greek transliteration of Zarathustra. If you're up on your German intellectual history, you know the name Zarathustra from Friedrich Nietzsche's great philosophical treatise *Also Sprach Zarathustra* or from Richard

Strauss's orchestral piece by the same name, which was taken from the title of Nietzsche's book. Despite the titles, neither Nietzsche's nor Strauss's work had much basis in the life and teachings of the historical Zarathustra, at least as far as I can tell.

In fact, precious little is known about Zoroaster beyond his name, so Nietzsche and Strauss didn't have much to work with. Most scholars agree that a biographical account of Zoroaster would be tenuous at best. There are many conflicting versions as to when and where he lived. Some research dates his birth to anywhere between 1500–1000 B.C.E. Mary Boyce, perhaps the leading scholar in this area of study, dates him to around 1200 B.C.E. But according to tradition, his birth date was 628 B.C.E., making him a near contemporary of the Buddha. Most current scholars would place him right at or somewhere before the start of Axial Age.

There is a general consensus that he lived in the eastern area of present day Iran, but some researchers would place him all the way back to Central Asia. We'll just have to live with these uncertainties. What *is* clear is that Zoroaster came from a modest family living in the semi-nomadic conditions of the Indo-Iranian times, as the cattle rustlers and outlaws were in their prime and druj seemed to be overwhelming asha.

Aside from much later traditions and legends, all the information we have about Zoroaster comes from a text that we call the Gathas, or the verses, which are part of the oldest Avesta, the foundational scripture of Zoroaster's religion. There are only 17 of these Gathas left, but there may have been more at one time. These verses are believed to have been actually composed by Zoroaster himself under moments of religious inspiration. They are written in an archaic dialect, very close to the language of the Sanskrit of the Rig Veda, and they're more spontaneous prayers addressed to god; they're not sermons or didactic proclamations.

The Gathas tell us Zoroaster was a priest. He calls himself a *zaotar,* one of the libation-pourers. As an authorized ritual specialist, Zoroaster would have been trained early in the priestly tradition and recognized as a full-fledged priest by the age of 15. I suspect it was his commitment to the rituals of his youth that prompted the transformation that led him eventually to assume the role of prophet and become the inspiration for the reform movement that became Zoroastrianism.

Prophet, by the way, is a different religious role from that of the priest. A priest usually functions as a mediator between humans and the divine: a prophet, by contrast, is often a critic of religious practices and functions as a mouthpiece for a god. Many think that Zoroaster may have been the world's first prophet in this sense.

Zoroaster was acutely aware of and troubled by the violence and lawlessness of the land. I can easily imagine the deep concern he may have felt over the way the old sacred rituals were now being pressed into the services of war and thieving. When we get to China later in the course, we'll observe how similar social circumstances quickened the moral conscience of Confucius, causing him to urge a renewed respect for religious ceremonies.

Zoroaster's moral sensitivities seem to have ultimately led him on a quest for deeper truths, much like the Buddha and many others who took to the wandering life to see the world in a clearer and more focused way in the Indian Axial Age. Tradition says that at age 30, Zoroaster had an impressive visionary experience at a river, in which he was led into the presence of the Ahura Mazda and six other radiant beings, who were known collectively as the *heptad* (that is, the "seven"), and there he received a special revelation. He left this luminous audience with a new sense of purpose, departing with the words, "I shall teach men to seek the right." The revelations do not stop here. Zoroaster has several more, but this was clearly the turning point in his life that transformed him from a mere priest to a prophet with a fire in the belly.

Before continuing with Zoroaster's career as a prophet, though, I want to take just a moment to make what I think is an interesting observation about the circumstances of his calling. The first is its location. It's fascinating to me how often such decisive revelations seem to occur by or in streams of water. The Hebrew prophet Ezekiel writes that while standing "by the river Chebar, the heavens were opened, and I saw visions of God." Jesus is baptized by John at the Jordan River, and hears the blessing of god the father, sees the vision of a dove, and begins preaching about the Kingdom of God. Guru Nanak, the founder of the Sikh movement in medieval India, is taken away into heaven for three days while bathing in a stream and then returns commissioned with a new message for Muslims and Hindus.

And, just as intriguing as the fact that these experiences occur to these individuals at the river, is the fact that they occur at the age of 30. Zoroaster, Ezekiel, Jesus, Nanak—and I could probably name a few more—were at this age when their critical revelations came. It's interesting. I'm not sure what to make of these observations, and I'm not going to detain us right now with speculation, but I will offer a thought or two when we get to the Buddha, who was near this age when he sets out for enlightenment. For now, just let me make a note of this cross-cultural feature, and forewarn those of you who may be approaching the age of thirty to be careful around streams and rivers. Strange things may happen to you.

Zoroaster's response to his new vocation was both conservative and revolutionary. As a traditionalist, he called his fellow Iranians to a simple return to respect for the principles of good, order, and harmony. But he added novel dimensions to this traditional worldview that made it an extremely powerful vision of the world.

There were two chief thrusts of Zoroaster's theology, both movements in the direction of simplification. First, Zoroaster became a passionate advocate for the worship of Ahura Mazda as the foremost deity. Zoroaster wanted Mazda to be seen as superior even to Varuna and the other ahuras. Even in his vision of the *heptad*, Zoroaster unmistakably saw Mazda as the dominant deity.

In later reflection and visions, Zoroaster seems to have refined this idea further, suggesting that the other ahuras and divinities were all just emanations or partial manifestations of Mazda. In Zoroaster's view, Mazda was the only uncreated god and the agent behind the seven-stage creation scheme that we discussed earlier. It would probably be too much to say that Zoroaster was a monotheist; but I think it's at least fair to say that his thinking certainly tended in this direction and probably helped contribute to the religious environment that would ultimately champion the monotheistic perspective.

Zoroaster's second innovation was to simplify the pantheon by assigning clear moral qualities to the gods. All the spirits—the *daevas*, the *ahuras*—were now plainly associated with either good or evil. Zoroaster removes any ambiguity. Because the *daevas* like Indra were honored by the cattle rustlers, whom Zoroaster called the Followers of the Lie, he reserved the word *daeva* exclusively for the wicked gods and the word ahura for the ethical gods.

By the way, the usage is still current in the west. Our word devil derives from the Iranian use of the word *daeva*. Now, let me note for clarification, that this usage only came down through Iran and not India. In India, the word *deva* does not hold this dichotomized association. *Devas* in India refer more to the power and status of divine beings and not specifically to their ethical nature. However, as if to return the favor to Zoroaster, the Indo-Aryans came to consider the *asuras*—the Sanskrit counterparts to the *ahuras*—as *evil* divinities. Zoroaster also used the term *yazatas*, to refer to the good spirits or divine assistants—not really gods as such—but beings associated with the principle of good and truth. The *yazatas* were probably the prototype for angels in the other western religions.

Consistent with this theological simplification, Zoroaster also suggested the existence of an independent evil deity, a chief god among the *daevas*. It is not certain, by any means, given the scant evidence, but Zoroaster may have in fact have been the first theologian in history to have conceived an autonomous, wholly evil supernatural being. In the Zoroastrian texts, this figure is called by various names including Aeshma and Angra Mainyu. He is more commonly called by his later name, Ahriman. Zoroaster thus envisioned two superior beings—one completely good and the other completely evil—locked in mortal combat since the beginning of time, each struggling for the triumph of his principles and powers.

In one of the ancient Gathas, we get a flavor of Zoroaster's worldview in a brief, and still rather cryptic, text called "The Two Spirits." The language, as I said, is archaic, and it's still not fully understood by modern scholars, but it does convey a sense for Zoroaster's theological perceptions.

> Now, these are the two original Spirits who, as twins, have been perceived [by me] through a vision. In both thought and speech, [and] in deed, these two are what is good and evil. Between these two, the pious, not the impious, will choose rightly.
>
> Furthermore, the two Spirits confronted each other; in the beginning [each] created for himself life and nonlife, so that in the end there will be the worst existence for the drujvants, but the best mind for the Righteous.

> Of these two Spirits, the deceitful (*drujvant*) chose the worst course of action, [while] the most beneficent Spirit who is clothed in the hardest stone [chose] Truth, [as] also [do] those who propitiate Ahura Mazda.
>
> Between these two [Spirits] the *daevas* did not choose wisely. While they were taking counsel among themselves, delusion came upon them, so that they choose the worst Mind. Then, all together, they ran to Wrath with which they infect the life of man.

This passage represents a lot of problems theologically. For instance, if Mazda were the original uncreated and wholly beneficent god, where did the evil spirit come from and why? Of course, that's the very problem of evil that has plagued the western traditions in religion for eons. Zoroaster doesn't attempt to solve the issue. What is more important for him is not the rather abstract issue of theological consistency, but the very pragmatic and existentially vital point that the human being has to make a choice between one or the other. Irrespective of the origins of these entities, human beings cannot escape the responsibility of aligning themselves with good or evil and must live their lives accordingly. Just as the *daevas* had made a choice, and ultimately made the wrong one, individual human beings are also confronted with the identical decision.

And this is one of the points where Zoroaster anticipates and perhaps partly instigates the transformations of the Axial Age. Time and again, as the course proceeds, we will encounter this call to make a choice, to align one's personal existence with the good or the evil, however conceived by the axial sages. It is a time when demands are being made on persons as individuals to accept responsibility for the moral quality of their actions and words.

In the post-Axial age, such claims on our lives might seem totally unremarkable. Well, of course, we must take moral responsibility for our decisions. But by and large, the call to this kind of personal obligation is novel in religious history, because it is connected with new ideas about what it means to be human and divine. Our continuing discussion on Zoroaster's reform and the influences it had will help verify my point. We'll see that for Zoroaster, the individual's moral and religious decisions now determine the quality of his or her personal destiny. One's future being, especially in the world beyond this one, depends on one's behavior here-and-now.

The idea is both new for the times and common in and across the Axial centers.

Lecture Four
Zoroaster's Legacy

Scope:

Zoroaster anticipated other Axial sages by connecting human destiny and moral behavior. He imagined human history moving in a linear fashion toward a final conclusion, in which good would at last triumph over evil. At this eschatological moment, those whose lives had been aligned with the Ahura Mazda, the god of good, would be rewarded with an everlasting life of happiness, while those who served Ahriman, the god of evil, would be utterly annihilated. Zoroaster's use of rituals, particularly those involving fire, was intended to help individuals cultivate moral qualities and ally with the spirit of good.

Although there are relatively few Zoroastrians left—today, it would not qualify as a major world religion—the legacy of Zoroaster's teachings lives on in other religions. Although a controversial issue, many scholars believe that the Western monotheisms—Judaism, Christianity, and Islam—absorbed some important aspects of Zoroastrian thought, such as the devil, the Day of Judgment, heaven and hell, angels, and the concept of a divine savior.

Outline

I. In simplifying Iranian religion, Zoroaster was both zealous prophet and great visionary, whose worldview was one of the most influential in history. His innovative theology helped shape other religious perspectives to come.

  A. Having clearly distinguished which gods were good and which were evil, Zoroaster's theology was simple: One had to choose between the two forces.

  B. Zoroaster also believed that one's ultimate destiny, in the afterlife, depended on whether one sided with the good Mazda or the evil Ahriman. This was a remarkable idea for its time because it suggested that individuals had a destiny beyond life. Earlier, such a belief was not widely accepted.

  C. Zoroaster claimed that the afterlife was dependent on one's moral behavior, which was counter to the popular belief of his day, that destiny depended on whether or not one had performed great deeds or pleased the gods with sufficient sacrifices. This *ethicization* is one of the great themes of the Axial transformation, the idea that beliefs and practices are interpreted and understood in moral terms.

D. Zoroaster believed that an individual would be judged on the fourth day following his or her death. Good people went to heaven to be with Mazda, while evil people fell into the abyss of hell.

II. Zoroaster also envisioned a final cosmic destiny in which all of humanity was headed in a particular direction.

A. He believed that time was linear, from beginning to apocalyptic end, which ultimately would result in a universal struggle between good and evil to be played out in a battle called Frashokereti, the "making glorious."

B. According to Zoroaster, good would prevail, establishing paradise on Earth.

C. Zoroaster may have believed in a bodily resurrection of the dead; those already in heaven would return to Earth and continue life in physical form.

D. He also expected a savior figure, a *saoshyant*, an apocalyptic judge who would play a decisive role in humanity's destiny.

E. It's unclear whether all of Zoroaster's ideas originated with him, but through his influence and prophecies, these ideas were widely disseminated.

III. What made Zoroaster's vision so compelling to many of his contemporaries?

A. First, it was incumbent upon individuals to make the essential good/evil choice, which determined one's future and shaped cosmic drama itself. The gods were at war, and human beings had to act to ensure that good prevailed. This elevated the importance of human moral responsibility.

B. Second, Zoroaster's vision provided meaning to suffering and promised compensation for it. For their suffering, the righteous would live an afterlife in paradise, while evil ones, too, received their just deserts.

C. Zoroaster spent his life preaching while missionaries spread his message. Many of his followers were persecuted and killed, but their martyrdom only strengthened the convictions of those who survived.

D. By the 6th century B.C.E., the movement became the state religion of the Achaemenid (Persian) Empire, which it remained until the 7th century C.E., when it was finally displaced by Islam.

IV. Zoroastrianism eventually developed rituals intended to reinforce its basic message and theology.

A. One central practice was to pray five times each day while standing before a fire, which could be the Sun or a fireplace. The Sun was associated with Mazda, and like their Indo-Aryan relatives, Iranians maintained the custom of keeping the sacred fires constantly lit.

B. Purity also became associated with fire rituals.

1. The constituent elements of the world—earth, fire, and water—needed to be kept pure.
2. To keep the soil pure, the dead were not buried. Instead, they were laid in "towers of silence," exposed for birds to pick their bones clean.
3. The purity code included the death penalty for anyone polluting a sacred fire, but it allowed the killing of snakes and scorpions, both believed to be demonic creatures.

C. Celebrations were also practiced, in particular seven major festivals tied to the rhythms of agricultural life. The most important was Noruz, or "New Day", a new year's celebration still held at the spring equinox, making it one of the oldest continuously celebrated festivals in the world.

V. Whether or not Zoroastrianism directly influenced three other major religions—Judaism, Christianity, and Islam—is a controversial issue. However, there are parallel beliefs among these religions, which all first began to appear in Jewish theology after the Exile, when Jews came into contact with the Persians.

A. Evidence of influence is difficult to prove conclusively. Although there are examples of borrowing from other scriptures in West Asia, there are none from Zoroastrianism.

B. Early Jewish and Christian theologians probably never read Zoroastrian scripture because much of it was in the oral tradition. The infiltration of Zoroastrian ideas most likely occurred as Jews came into contact with followers of the movement during the post-Exile period.

   1. In the 6th century B.C.E., Jews came into contact with the Persian Empire; thereafter, new ideas—curiously similar to Zoroaster's—began to appear in Jewish and, later, Christian writings.

   2. These ideas were significantly different from the theology of earlier Hebrew writings and bear the traces of outside influences.

C. One of the parallels among these religions is the linear view of time, with a beginning, middle, and end.

D. Another parallel is the belief in a final apocalypse. The idea of the Day of Judgment first appeared in the books of Ecclesiastes and Daniel; the latter vision has the same Zoroastrian themes of an apocalyptic end to history, a resurrection of bodies and a day of judgment, and the determination of human destiny based on the moral quality of the individual's life.

E. A third parallel is the belief in heaven and hell and the idea that human beings might attain everlasting life in the heavenly realm or experience anguish in hell.

F. The idea of the devil seems clearly to be of Iranian origin. The devil appears nowhere in Genesis, but by the time the New Testament was written, 500–600 years after the Exile, Satan emerged as a god of evil.

G. A final important parallel among these religions is the idea of a universal savior or apocalyptic judge who appears at the end times.

   1. Though the idea of a messiah was part of Jewish tradition before Jewish contact with the Persians, their vision of the messiah, who he was and what his role might be, was far from clear.

2. Zoroaster's idea of a *saoshyant*, a universal redeemer appearing at the end times, may have shaped some of the Jews' expectations. An apocalyptic figure called the Son of Man first appears in Daniel, in which we read that this figure would descend from heaven at the end of history and play a decisive role in the annihilation of evil.

H. Finally, it is possible that the wise men who appeared at Jesus' birth were actually Zoroastrians searching for their *saoshyant* and were led to Judea, where Jesus was born.

Essential Reading:

Foltz, *Spirituality in the Land of the Noble*, chapters 3 and 5.

Supplementary Reading:

Hultgård, "Persian Apocalypticism."

Questions to Consider:

1. What was revolutionary about Zoroaster's thought?
2. Why might some people be uncomfortable with the idea that Zoroastrianism influenced primary notions in Judaism, Christianity, and Islam? If you are a Jew, Christian, or Muslim, does the idea that Zoroastrianism may have contributed some important beliefs to your religion affect your faith?
3. How is life different if time is conceived as cyclical rather than linear?

Lecture Four—Transcript

Zoroaster's Legacy

Zoroaster was both a zealous prophet calling for a return to old-time religion as well as a great visionary with startling new ideas. The result of these qualities was a compelling worldview that was one of the most influential in history. In terms of its effects on other religions, Zoroastrianism may well have had the *greatest* impact of any single religion in the world. In the next half hour, we will continue to explore the novel aspects of Zoroaster's theology and suggest the ways his innovations directly and indirectly shaped other religious perspectives.

Zoroaster had greatly simplified Iranian religion. Everything came down to a simple, uncomplicated choice: Are you on the side of good or evil? He had already made clear which powers were good and which evil. All that remained was for the individual human being to make a choice, the same way the divine beings had.

But to this simple choice, Zoroaster added another element. Zoroaster believed that the individual's ultimate destiny depended on the choice he or she made. How he arrived at this conclusion is far from clear, but he was convinced that one's final end as a human being depended on whether one sided with the wholly good Mazda or the wholly evil Ahriman. I doubt many of you gasped with astonishment when I made that statement. The idea is such a commonplace notion that it seems almost totally unremarkable. Virtually every major religion makes a similar claim. What ultimately becomes of you—whether you go to heaven as in Christianity, or paradise in Islam, or find nibbana in Buddhism, or moksha in Hinduism—is contingent on the moral and theological choices that you make here and now.

But in the pre-Axial age, this *was* a remarkable idea. The first unusual thing about it is it suggested that the individual human in fact has a destiny beyond this life. Prior to the Axial Age, such belief was not widely accepted. Some may have held that prominent individuals like the king enjoyed some kind of post-mortem existence. But even these ideas were rarely well defined and thought out. With the advent of the Axial Age, the view that individuals might have a destiny in a hereafter came to be more widely accepted.

But even more unusual was Zoroaster's claim that those prospects were dependent on one's moral choices. Even in those cultures that held to some kind of belief in an afterlife, almost never was destiny contingent on moral behavior. One's after-death future might be predicated on ritual practices—whether or not one had pleased the gods with sacrifices of sufficient quantity and quality, or perhaps on the performance of great deeds, such as heroism in a great battle. But rarely ever do we find the claim before the Axial period that the individual's destiny is determined by moral decisions. This, in fact, is one of the great themes of the Axial transformation, and one to which we'll return. For clarity's sake, we'll refer to this motif as ethicization, the process whereby certain beliefs and practices are interpreted and understood in moral terms. In the view of Zoroaster, then, we can say the future of the human being has been ethicized.

Zoroaster believed that individuals would be judged on the fourth day following their death. He imagined that that judgment would take place at High Hara, the first and most sacred mountain on earth, where the great ahuras had their palaces. Those individuals found to be good were led to the heavens across a wide bridge accompanied by a beautiful maiden, who was a reflection of their own inner goodness. In the heavens, they enjoyed the company of Mazda and the other ashavans. Those who were judged evil had to cross an extremely narrow bridge—the texts say the width of a razor's edge—and were led by a revolting hag. Inevitably, they fell while crossing and landed in the abyss of hell, where they suffered painfully for their sins in the realm ruled by the Evil One.

But the story doesn't end here. The assignment to heaven or hell was ultimately only a temporary one. Zoroaster also envisioned a final cosmic destiny. As Zoroaster saw it, history—not just individual people, but history itself—was headed in a particular direction. Unlike his contemporaries around the world, Zoroaster saw time moving in a linear fashion, from a beginning to an apocalyptic conclusion. The end of the world, he thought, would come as the universal struggle between good and evil came to a head. He thought this final conflict would end in a spectacular battle that he called the Frashokereti, the "making glorious." In this war to end all wars, Zoroaster had no doubt that good would prevail and evil utterly and forever banished from existence. The Evil One, his minions, hell, and all its human inhabitants would be annihilated, and paradise would be established on earth. Zoroaster may have connected this vision with a bodily resurrection of the dead, in which those who had initially gone to heaven now returned to earth to continue life in physical form. If this were Zoroaster's belief, he would have been among the first—if not *the* first—to have conceptualized such a fate.

Zoroaster also seems to have expected a savior or an apocalyptic judge figure who would appear at the Frashokereti and play a decisive role in it. The ancient Avestan texts refer to this future redeemer as a *saoshyant*. According to Zoroastrian prophecy, the Saoshyant would be born from a virgin who had become pregnant by bathing in a lake in which Zoroaster's semen had been miraculously preserved.

These concepts—a grand cosmic struggle between good and evil, history moving towards a final conclusion, the appearance of a redeemer-judge, the resurrection of the dead, and the call for humans to choose sides—all constitute Zoroaster's novel ideas. We can't say for certain that all these ideas originated with him; perhaps he was in conversation with like-minded persons or with ancient traditions. But we can say that it was through Zoroaster's influence and prophetic message that these ideas were widely disseminated among the Iranians.

Let's take a moment to appreciate what made this vision so compelling to many of Zoroaster's contemporaries. First, Zoroaster's vision implied a decisive role for human beings. To Zoroaster, people were not the pawns of the gods. The gods did not intervene and fool with the lives of hapless humans. Persons had a choice to make, and that choice was essential. It determined the individual's future and it shaped the cosmic drama itself. The gods were at war, and human beings had to act to ensure the side of right prevailed. In this way, Zoroaster greatly elevated the importance of human moral responsibility.

But equally important is the way Zoroaster's vision provided meaning to human suffering and promised ultimate compensation for it. Those suffering from an unkind fate, from thieves and the cattle rustlers, from illness and deprivation could see their plight in a much larger context. Their anguish and misery was part of a grand drama involving the entire world and was not just bad luck or random happenstance. For their suffering, the righteous would be given ample reparations. Immortal life in paradise—free of any and all evil—would suffice to make earthly suffering seem insignificant by comparison. And they could be satisfied by the sense that the evil ones, too, would receive their just deserts.

Well, despite the compelling nature of Zoroaster's theology, the Gathas say that Zoroaster was not well received in his own community, a fate that he shared with Jesus and Muhammad. Soon after his rejection, Zoroaster moved to another location and obtained some success in gathering followers there, with the patronage of influential persons in the area. He spent the rest of his life preaching and sending missionaries to spread his message of Mazda worship.

Proselytizing, by the way, was extremely uncommon in the pre-Axial world. Eventually, his message spread throughout west Asia and as far east as China. Because many experienced his message as a threat, many of his followers were persecuted and killed. The persecutions, however, merely convinced Zoroaster's followers of the truth of their convictions and it effectively strengthened the movement. By the 6th century B.C.E., the movement had amassed enough power to function as the state religion of the Persian Empire, and remained the state religion of two subsequent Iranian empires until the 7th century C.E., when it was finally displaced by Islam.

The various rituals of Zoroastrianism were intended to enforce its basic message and theology. Zoroaster prescribed one central practice for all of his followers: prayer five times each day. The Indo-Iranians were already accustomed to praying three times a day: Zoroaster added prayer at dawn and midnight to this routine. For the followers of Zoroaster, prayer was to be performed while standing in the presence of fire. The fire might be the sun if one were outdoors, or the fireplace if in the home. The sun had by now come to be closely associated with Ahura Mazda. Like their Indo-Aryan relatives, the Iranians maintained the custom of keeping the sacred fires constantly lit. Some Muslims later criticized the Zoroastrians as fire-worshippers, and they're still sometimes called that sometimes in places like India, where they are known as the Parsis. Zoroastrians, of course, resent the fire worshipper label since they understand themselves to be worshiping god, and not the fire.

Fire rituals were actually part of Zoroastrian purity practice. Purity was extremely important to the Iranians, just as it was to the Indo-Aryans. According to Zoroaster, the constituent elements of the world—earth, fire, and especially water—needed to be kept clean and uncontaminated. The Zoroastrians actually gave up burial of the dead for fear of contaminating the soil, and instead placed corpses in "towers of silence, exposed to the air to let the birds of prey pick the bones clean. The Zoroastrian purity code also included the penalty of death for anyone polluting a sacred fire. Yet at the same time, it allowed for the killing of snakes and scorpions, both believed to be demonic animals in league with the *daevas*.

The Zoroastrians celebrated seven major festivals, tied mainly to the rhythms of agricultural life. By far, the most important was new year's, which the Iranians called Noruz, and it was celebrated at the spring equinox. Noruz means "New Day". New Day is still widely celebrated by Iranians, and in Pakistan, Afghanistan, and parts of India, and is still one of the oldest continuously celebrated festivals on earth. Noruz is intended to anticipate the overthrow of the evil ones at the end time and so it is a very joyous celebration.

If you are acquainted with the three great traditions of the west—Judaism, Christianity, and Islam—much of Zoroaster's theology must sound familiar. Surely you've wondered whether the parallels among these traditions are merely coincidental or whether there has been some actual historical influence from one tradition to the others. This has been, and still is, a controversial issue. Many Jews, Christians, and Muslims deny or minimize the significance of the parallels, believing that such comparisons somehow detract from the uniqueness or divine origin of their religion. Nonetheless, most scholars working in this area are convinced that formative Judaism, Christianity, and Islam were shaped directly or indirectly by the more ancient Zoroastrian beliefs.

This influence, however, is difficult to document and prove conclusively because the case is based largely on circumstantial evidence. There are no passages in the Bible or the Qur'an that quote from the Gathas or even paraphrase it. While there are examples of such borrowing from other scriptures in West Asia, there is none from Zoroastrianism. Early Jewish and Christian theologians probably never read any of the Zoroastrian scriptures because most of Zoroaster's religion remained in oral tradition for centuries. The infiltration of Zoroastrian ideas most likely occurred in a much less formal way as Jews came into contact with Zoroastrian practitioners and engaged them in conversation and observed their practices.

Although circumstantial, the case for Zoroastrian influence still seems persuasive to me, and the argument's a simple one: In the 6th century B.C.E., during the formative period of Judaism, Jews came into contact with the Persian Empire during and after the Exile, or Babylonian Captivity, and thereafter, new ideas—curiously like Zoroaster's—began to appear in Jewish and then later Christian writings. These ideas were significantly different from the theology of earlier Hebrew writings and bear the traces of outside influences.

I won't have the time to examine all of these ideas in great detail, but I'll mention the principal ones and then explore two or three in more detail. The first is the linear view of time, the idea that cosmic history has a beginning, a middle, and an end. This concept is often contrasted with the more common view of time as cyclical, as constantly repeating itself, but ultimately going nowhere, a view that we'll encounter when we get to India. The key element to the linear understanding of history is the idea of an end time. Although there were vague intimations of an eschaton, or an end time, in Jewish writings prior to the Exile, it's only afterwards that this theme began to dominate Jewish thought and was accepted as mainstream Jewish theology. And it was most often connected with the idea of a final apocalypse, the end of history brought about by a grand showdown between good and evil and ending in the final judgment of human beings according to their deeds.

The idea of a Day of Judgment did not appear in Jewish theology until the post-Exilic period. The first appearance of this idea in the Bible was in the books of Ecclesiastes and Daniel, both written after the Jewish contact with the Persian world. The book of Ecclesiastes ends with this verse: "For God will bring every deed into judgment, including every secret thing, whether good or evil." The book of Daniel is even more explicit:

> There shall be a time of anguish, such as has never occurred since nations came into existence. But at that time your people shall be delivered, everyone whose name is found written in the book. Many of those who sleep in the dust of the earth shall awake, some to everlasting life, and some to shame and … contempt. Those who are wise shall shine like the brightness of the sky, and those who lead many to righteousness, like the stars forever and ever.

We hear in these words of Daniel's vision the same Zoroastrian themes of an apocalyptic end to history, a resurrection of bodies and a day of judgment, and the determination of human destiny based on the moral quality of the individual's life.

After the Exile, we also see for the first time in Jewish thought the ideas of heaven and hell as ultimate destinations for human beings; the belief in angels and demons, and the concepts of a universal savior and the devil. Now obviously, the Bible speaks of heaven from the start of Genesis, but throughout most of the Bible, heaven is simply meant the realm of the divine, the place the gods inhabited. The idea that human beings might attain everlasting life in the heavenly realm was simply foreign to Jewish thinking prior to the Exile.

The shades, the residue of individuals were believed to descend to an underworld known as *Sheol* where they continued a shadowy, quasi-existence. Descent to *Sheol* was simply in the nature of things; it didn't depend in any way on one's moral character. But after Persian contact, Jewish thinkers increasingly conceived of an afterlife in either heaven or hell, now understood as paradise or perdition, respectively. In fact, the word paradise, which the later books of the Bible use as synonymous with heaven, derives from the ancient Iranian words *pairi-daeza*, which means enclosed garden.

The idea of the devil, which came to figure more prominently in Christianity than Judaism, seems quite clearly to be of Iranian origin. The closest thing to a devil in the Hebrew Bible is in the Book of Job. Contrary to the impression of many, the devil appears nowhere in the story of Adam and Eve, or anywhere else in Genesis. Even in the Book of Job, the figure called the Satan is not really the same character that goes by that name in the New Testament. In the story of Job, the Satan—which is a title rather than a name—was a member of the heavenly court who tries to keep God honest in a way by challenging him to a wager involving a righteous man. In no sense does the Satan appear as a wholly malevolent deity or even as the embodiment of evil. In fact, as I read Job, God and the Satan seem to be on pretty friendly—if somewhat adversarial—terms.

But by the time the New Testament was written, some 500-600 years after the Babylonian exile, Satan emerged as a god of evil, living in hell, and constantly assaulting the people of God, just like Ahriman.

Jesus speaks a great deal of the devil and the New Testament portrays the two confronting one another. Jesus' death and resurrection is even interpreted as breaking the power of the devil over humanity. Some centuries after Jesus, the Christian theologian Augustine argued that Satan was once one of God's spiritual creatures who chose to be evil out of pride. At this point, it is hard to distinguish the Christian view of Satan from Zoroaster's concept of the Evil One, and it is equally hard to resist the conclusion that the latter decisively contributed to the former.

There is one idea that must be mentioned, and that is the belief in the universal savior or apocalyptic judge who appears at the end of time. The expectation of a messiah, of course, had been a part of the Jewish tradition for a long time, and I think there are clear indications that these expectations began to emerge even before the Jews had contact with Zoroastrian theology. But the Jewish expectations for the messiah were far from clear or monolithic. Messiah, which simply means anointed one, was used to refer to individuals such as King David and even Cyrus, the Persian king who freed the Jews from their Babylonian captivity.

By the time of Jesus, the expectation of a messiah was rife among the Jews, but there seemed to be no consensus as to who this figure was supposed to be or what he was supposed to do. But Zoroaster's idea of a *saoshyant*, a universal redeemer who appears at the end time, may have shaped some of the Jews' expectations. In the post-Exilic book of Daniel, we read for the first time about an apocalyptic figure called the Son of Man who would descend from heaven at the end of history and play a decisive role in the annihilation of evil and return the world to the path of righteousness. Daniel writes of his vision:

> I saw one like a [Son of Man] coming with the clouds of heaven.
>
> And he came to the Ancient One and was presented before him.
>
> To him was given dominion and glory and kingship, that all the peoples, nations, and languages should serve him. His dominion is an everlasting dominion that shall not pass away, and his kingship is one that shall never be destroyed.

Jesus frequently referred to himself as the Son of Man, particularly in Mark, the earliest gospel. There is debate, of course, on what he may have meant when he used that title, but I think it's at least plausible that he believed his role in ushering in the kingdom of god would be his post-crucifixion appearance as the end-time redeemer and judge. But whether or not they believed Jesus was the one, it is clear that many Jews expected a messiah whose role would be like that of the Saoshyant.

Finally, it is with respect to Jesus that we have at least one biblical reference to the religion of the Zoroastrians. The Gospel of Matthew mentions that a year or two after Jesus' birth, wise men "from the East," who had been studying the stars, came to visit and pay their respects. These wise men were called the magi. It's a Greek word based on the Persian word *magus*, the Old Persian term for priest. Matthew's story now takes on added richness when we consider that these eastern visitors may have been Zoroastrians who were scanning the heavens for signs of their Saoshyant and were led to Judea where Jesus was born.

Although there's much more to be said about Zoroaster and his religion, and the impact he had on world religion, we must draw this discussion to a close. I hope I've said some things that will pique your curiosity enough to pursue some of these issues on your own.

When we return, we'll pick up with the history of the other side of this great clan, as we observe the migration of the Indo-Aryans into south Asia. I'll see you then.

Lecture Five
South Asia before the Axial Age

Scope:

From Iran, we move to South Asia and the pre-Axial culture of what came to be India. We first examine the indigenous Indus Valley culture, whose religious practices focused on goddess worship and fertility rituals. Then we witness the migration of the Indo-Aryans, the descendants of the Indo-Iranians who found their way to South Asia. Although no one is quite sure what occurred when the Indo-Aryans encountered the Indus culture—or what was left of it—the meeting of these traditions yielded profound changes for Indian religion and ultimately provided the basis for the Hindu family of religions. The Indo-Aryans brought with them a worldview and a set of rituals based on their revealed scriptures, the Vedas. Through those texts, we glimpse the Aryan pantheon of gods and their understanding of human beings.

Outline

I. To help us understand the transformations that led to the birth of the Axial religions of India, we look at the Indus culture, which flourished along the Indus River valley at least 1,500 years before the Indo-Aryans entered what is now Pakistan and the Punjab area.

A. By the time the Aryans arrived in the region, around 1500 B.C.E., the Indus culture was declining but still potent enough to influence the evolution of Hinduism, believed to have emerged from the confluence of the ancient Indo-Aryan and Indus religions.

B. The Indus culture was discovered in the 19th century when ruins were found, indicating that this was the largest civilization of the ancient world, with some cities containing as many as 50,000 people at one time.

C. We know little about the Indus dwellers' governance and society, but evidence suggests a centralized authority and law enforcement.

D. They were likely peaceful agriculturists who traded with the Mesopotamians.

E. The Indus language remains indecipherable; thus, we don't know what these people called themselves and have no writings to aid in our understanding of their religion.

II. Indus dwellers were deeply concerned with sexuality and procreation. Archeological finds include figurines of women with exaggerated hips and breasts. Horned animals with powerful flanks and obvious male genitalia depict male sexuality. However, without textual evidence, we can make only educated guesses about these artifacts based on similar findings in other societies.

A. Female figurines are thought to symbolize a divine goddess, indicating that the earliest humans worshiped a mother goddess long before male gods.

1. Whether or not Indus dwellers were part of a vast goddess religion, they did revere and celebrate the reproductive powers of women.

2. Goddess worship is a prominent part of contemporary Hinduism, with a long and deep-rooted history, and it's plausible that this tradition derives from Indus practices.

B. The depiction of horned male animals and stone phalluses implies a fascination with sexuality and reproductive functions. But what precisely was the icons' function?

1. Throughout recorded history, Hindus revered a god, Shiva, represented symbolically as the male and female sex organs in an icon called the *lingam-yoni*, alluding to the powers of creation and procreation and the importance of male/female balance.

2. Indus images may have functioned in much the same way as the modern Shiva, thus revering creative power and balance.

C. Sexual images might have had a magical function, such as good luck charms to enhance fertility and conception.

III. Indus cities also had sophisticated bathing facilities, suggesting an intense concern with purity and cleanliness beyond simple hygiene. But as yet, no obvious places of worship or sacred precincts have been unearthed.

A. Like Hindus today, the Indus peoples seemed focused on ritual purity, or cleanliness necessary for approaching the sacred. Ritual purity also concerns food, clothing, the persons one may touch or associate with, and a host of similar regulations and restrictions.

B. Purity rituals maintained a society's sense of order; thus, the baths likely served to remove impurities and reinstate the order of things, just as in contemporary Hinduism.

C. Because no positively identified sacred buildings have yet been unearthed in the Indus culture, the home may have served as a sacred space, again, similar to contemporary Hinduism. This underscores the important pre-Axial fact that the sacred and secular were not sharply distinguished.

D. There is no indication that the Indus peoples thought much about an afterlife. Ritual practices seemed to be chiefly for maintaining order in the present.

IV. Already in decline by 1500 B.C.E., the Indus culture came to an end at about the time that the "Indo" branch of the Indo-Iranian people began to arrive in the region.

A. Formerly, historians believed that the Indo-Aryans conquered the Indus culture. But many contemporary scholars of ancient India think that the Indo-Aryans migrated slowly and relatively peacefully into the Indus region, coexisting for a time with the remaining Indus peoples.

B. Some scholars contend that the Aryans were actually indigenous to India, not Central Asia, and migrated from the subcontinent to other locations. Regardless of where they originated, ancient connections can be found between the Indo-Aryans and the Iranians.

C. Initially, the Indo-Aryans were pastoral nomads, not agriculturalists. They called themselves the "Five Tribes" and were led by chieftains. Recall that the Indo-Aryans also referred to themselves as the "Noble Ones," the literal meaning of *Aryan*.

V. Our knowledge of the Aryans comes from the Vedas, instructions, prayers, and hymns created for the purpose of performing rituals.

A. Today, the Vedas are the Hindus' oldest and most sacred scripture of divine knowledge with universal secrets.

B. The Vedas are divided into four collections. The oldest, and the one we'll look at, is the Rig Veda, which contains more than 1,000 songs to various gods and goddesses.

C. The Vedas tell us that Aryan religion principally involved ritual and sacrifice. As in Indus culture, Aryan ritual appears to focus mainly on acquiring the necessary goods for a happy and comfortable existence in the present.

VI. To understand the Aryans, we explore some of their rituals, why they were performed, and to whom they were addressed.

A. The Vedas describe 33 different gods and goddesses believed to dwell on Earth, in heaven, and in the mid-space between the two worlds, a tripartite world similar to that envisioned by the Iranians.

B. Most of these gods—*devas* in the Sanskrit—had specific functions or realms.

1. For instance, Indra was the god of war and, according to Zoroaster, was one of the principal *devas* associated with chaos and evil.

2. Agni was the divine fire who lived in the domestic hearth and in plants. He also dwelled in mid-space as lightning and as the fire of the Sun. Because of his versatility, Agni was the mediator between gods and humans and, therefore, figured prominently in Aryan rituals.

3. Other gods and goddesses included Surya (Sun), Yama (death), Ushas (dawn), Kubera (wealth and prosperity), and a host of other, lesser divine beings of different ranks and qualities, including the *asuras*, whom the Indo-Aryans considered evil.

C. Different *devas* took center stage at varying times and were usually worshiped according to whose favors were needed at the moment.

VII. We now look at how the Indo-Aryans viewed themselves

and their place in the universe.

A. Significantly, the Vedas have very little to say about views of human nature and destiny. Aryans rarely analyzed themselves nor had they a systematic self-understanding.

B. The Vedas are more interested in praising gods and performing rituals than understanding what it means to be human.

C. The Rig Veda hymns portray fairly wide speculation about what occurs at death. One hymn alone lists numerous possible fates for humans, from going to heaven, to dissolving into the elements of the natural world, to being "cooked" by the funeral pyre and subsequently consumed by the gods.

   1. Other hymns suggest that the soul descends to the underworld, ruled by Yama.

   2. The hymns contain no consensus about the makeup of the human personality or about what determines one's final destiny.

D. The Aryan relationship to the body is not spelled out, and it's unclear what determines fate.

   1. Sometimes, it appears that the correct performance of rituals decides one's destiny; sometimes, it seems to depend on deeds; and sometimes, one's fate is unrelated to the life lived.

   2. The Vedas make no pronouncements that destiny is related to moral choices, as Zoroaster believed.

E. The Aryans surely regarded death as an occasion for grief and sadness, yet there is no indication that death was terrifying or that an afterlife—if there was one—was unpleasant.

F. The Rig Veda also says nothing of reincarnation, an Axial development that receives widespread acceptance as the Vedic tradition evolves into Hinduism.

Essential Reading:

Hopkins, *The Hindu Religious Tradition*, chapter 1.

Supplementary Reading:

O'Flaherty, *The Rig-Veda*, "Creation," "Agni," "Indra," "Varuna."

Questions to Consider:

1. What are the similarities between the Indus culture and contemporary Hindu tradition?
2. What are some of the differences between Indus peoples' beliefs and Zoroastrianism?

Lecture Five—Transcript
South Asia before the Axial Age

It's now time to move toward South Asia, and especially the area we now know as India. Almost half the lectures in this series will be dedicated to this region, simply because so much happened there during the Axial Age. In coming lectures, we'll discuss the evolution of Hinduism, Buddhism, and Jainism. But today, we start with a sketch of India prior to the Axial ferment to help us understand the transformations that led to the birth of these religions.

We are already familiar with a major part of the pre-Axial Indian world from our conversations on the Indo-Iranian peoples, who migrated from the Central Asian steppes before finally splitting up and going separate ways. We spent a fair amount of time exploring the religious world of the Indo-Iranians, the world that they held in common prior to their division. With this lecture, we begin to turn our attention to the development of this tradition through the Indo-Aryans who ultimately settled in India. Just as the tradition that developed in Iran assumed new forms and made significant departures from the ancient common religion, so too the Indo-Aryan tradition changed in diverse and novel ways, especially when it entered its new homeland.

But before we take up the Indo-Aryan migration into India, we must first consider another civilization that occupied this territory prior to their arrival. Long before the Indo-Aryans entered the northwestern part of the subcontinent—the region of the present state of Pakistan and the area known as the Punjab—a major civilization flourished there. The Indus Culture, as it's now called, was situated along the Indus River system and existed at least 1,500 years before the Indo-Aryans appeared. By the time the Aryans settled in this area, around 1500 B.C.E., this civilization was in decline. Yet its vestiges were still potent enough to profoundly influence the evolution of Hinduism. Today, scholars generally believe that the Hindu traditions emerged out of the confluence of the ancient Indo-Aryan and Indus culture religions.

Up until the middle of the 19th century, the Indus civilization had been completely forgotten by humanity. It wasn't until the 19th century, when British engineers were excavating, that they accidentally uncovered the ruins of this culture. Before that time, modern humanity had no idea that there had ever been an Indus civilization. Today, we know this civilization was the largest of the ancient world. So far, archaeologists have uncovered over 70 cities in an area about the size of Texas. These urban centers were remarkably well planned and organized. The largest may have contained as many as 50,000 inhabitants at one time.

We know very little about the way Indus dwellers governed themselves or structured their society, but the uniformity of their cities suggest some kind of centralized authority and law enforcement. And we can infer from the absence of any significant weapons among the archaeological artifacts that the Indus civilization was relatively peaceful. We also know that agriculture was the basis of their economy along with trade with other cultures, most notably the Mesopotamians living along the Tigris and Euphrates rivers.

What we do not know is their language. We have plenty of examples of Indus writing, but as yet scholars have been unable to decipher it. Thus, we have no idea what the citizens of this great society called themselves, and we have no literary methods for understanding Indus religion. Our present knowledge is essentially informed speculation based on the material artifacts of the ruins. There is simply no textual evidence to help corroborate or refute scholarly inferences.

We can say with some confidence that the Indus dwellers were deeply concerned with the functions of sexuality and procreation, and that this preoccupation was reflected in their religious practices. Throughout the region, archaeologists have uncovered a large number of terracotta figurines of women with exaggerated hips and large breasts. Interestingly, we found no corresponding portrayals of men as icons of sexuality. Rather, to depict male sexuality, Indus artisans created images of horned animals—such as bulls and buffaloes—with very powerful flanks and rather obvious male genitalia. In addition to these representations, excavations have turned up a large array of stone and clay phalluses and vulvas, whose precise function is not certain.

Without textual evidence, we can only make some educated guesses about these artifacts, based on similar findings in other societies and in later Hinduism. So here is some informed speculation. Female figurines, similar to those of the Indus Valley, have been unearthed in various parts of the world and are thought to symbolize a divine woman or goddess. Some researchers argue that these images indicate the earliest humans worshiped a mother goddess long before the male gods. If so, perhaps the Indus dwellers were part of this vast goddess religion.

But the idea of a pervasive goddess religion is still a controversial one and not all scholars agree on it. Yet it does seem evident that—at least in the Indus Culture—the reproductive powers of women were revered and celebrated, and perhaps women themselves were regarded as sacred. One certain thing is that the worship of the goddess is a prominent part of contemporary Hinduism and has a long, and deep-rooted, history. It seems entirely reasonable to believe that this Hindu tradition derives from these Indus practices.

Obviously, the depiction of horned male animals and stone phalluses also imply a fascination with—or perhaps an anxiety about—sexuality and reproductive functions. But what precisely was their function? Here, historical and current religious practices may give us some clues. Throughout their recorded history, Hindus have revered a god known as Shiva, who has been represented symbolically as the male and female sex organs in an icon called the *lingam-yoni*. The meaning of this representation is very rich, and it alludes to the generative powers of creation and procreation, as well as to the importance of balance between male and female.

The stone and clay images found in the Indus culture may have functioned in much the same way as the modern representations of Shiva, providing a focus for revering these principles of creative power and balance. It's also possible that these sexual images had a magical function. In some cultures, carved phalluses are used like good luck charms to enhance fertility and conception. It's plausible that the dwellers of the Indus Valley may have used such carvings in similar ways to magically help facilitate the reproductive process. We moderns sometimes forget how for most of human history the process of reproduction was an extremely mysterious thing.

Throughout the Indus cities, in public places and private homes, there were also sophisticated bathing facilities, plumbed and lined with ceramic tiles in a relatively modern way. The ubiquity of the baths, and their central locations, and the care with which they were constructed all suggest an intense concern with purity and cleanliness. Almost certainly, this concern was with more than simple hygiene.

Like many pre-modern cultures, and like Hindus today, the Indus dwellers were probably concerned with ritual purity. Ritual purity, as compared to hygienic purity, involves more than just removing the sweat and grime that accumulates on the body and avoiding germs that cause disease. In its most basic sense, ritual purity is the state of cleanliness that is necessary for approaching the sacred. It often concerns what and how one eats, the kinds of clothes one wears, the persons one may touch or associate with, and a host of similar regulations and restrictions. Such rules, of course, vary from culture to culture, but essentially they all concern maintaining a society's sense of order. Whenever that order is violated—whether intentionally or unintentionally—it is necessary to restore it.

We do not know specifically what kinds of things the Indus dwellers regarded as ritually impure. Whatever it may have been, the baths most likely served to remove those impurities and to reinstate the order of things, just as it does in contemporary Hinduism. In modern India, the first religious act of the day for most Hindus is bathing, a ritual practice that brings the individual into the appropriate bodily and mental state for relating to the gods and to other persons.

Perhaps as important as what archaeologists have uncovered around the Indus is what they have failed to find. As yet, no temple or house of worship has been found that can be positively identified as a sacred precinct. It may be that the central location of religion for this culture was the home, as it is in present-day Hinduism. But in any event, the absence of a clearly recognizable temple underscores an important fact of pre-Axial existence throughout the world: that sacred and secular, or the holy and the profane, are not sharply distinguished. There was no separate domain of life that could be identified as religious.

So, the Indus culture adds a few strokes to our emerging portrait of life in pre-Axial India. As best we can discern with our current knowledge, we can see that prior to the Axial Age, many Indians were especially concerned with sexuality and reproduction, and that concern probably encompassed the human, the animal, and the plant realms, as would be customary for an agricultural society. And in all likelihood, this fascination and anxiety implicated the divine realm.

Perhaps a mother goddess, and maybe animals themselves, were worshiped to help ensure fertility and fecundity on all levels of life. And finally, the design of cities and the practices of ritual purity indicate a deep concern with order and restraint.

To the extent that this is an accurate sketch of Indus religion, it suggests that beliefs and practices were oriented towards the present life here on earth and not towards a life hereafter. There is nothing in the ruins that indicate that Indus dwellers thought much about an afterlife or even wondered about what might be in store for the individual on the other side of death. Ritual practices and sacrifices seemed to be exclusively, if not chiefly, for the purposes of maintaining order in the here-and-now. Religion served a conservative function in this culture: to keep things as they are; and to maintain the world by honoring and harnessing its powers and respecting its boundaries. And for a millennium and a half, the Indus religion was quite successful at doing that. Little seems to have changed during this civilization during its 1,500-year lifespan.

But, obviously, the Indus culture came to an end, probably because of gradual environmental changes. The details are still unclear, but the Indus Culture was in serious decline by 1500 B.C.E. It was about this time, maybe a little before, that the Indo branch of the Indo-Iranian people began to filter into the Indus River valley.

For many years, historians believed that the Indo-Aryans invaded the Indus culture and conquered its inhabitants. This was not an unreasonable conclusion, given the Aryans' love for war and conquest. This belief, in fact, informed Adolf Hitler's appropriation of the Aryan myth and the swastika, which was an ancient Aryan symbol. Today, most students of ancient India think the Aryans' arrival in India was well short of an invasion. Probably the Indo-Aryans migrated slowly and relatively peacefully into the Indus region and may have coexisted for a time with the remaining citizens of the Indus culture.

I should point out, however, that the so-called "Aryan question" is the subject of great debate currently. Some scholars and traditional Hindus contend that the Aryans were actually indigenous to India, not Central Asia, and migrated from the subcontinent to other locations. Unfortunately, we haven't the time to embark on a discussion of that issue, though it certainly merits attention. Obviously, I have presented a different view of the migration. But regardless from where the Aryans originated, there is little doubt that there are ancient connections between the Indo-Aryans and the Iranians.

As we know, the Indo-Aryans were initially pastoral nomads rather than settled agriculturalists. By the time they entered India, they were skilled in horsemanship, the use of chariots, and manufacturing bronze. They organized themselves into tribes led by chieftains and often referred to themselves as the Five Tribes. But their favorite self-designation—you'll recall—was the "Noble Ones," the literal meaning of *Aryan*. From this point on in our discussion of India, instead of the compound Indo-Aryan, I'll sometimes simply use the term Aryan, since that is how they referred to themselves. There's no need at this point to distinguish the Indo-Aryans from the Irano-Aryans, or the Iranians.

The basis of our knowledge of the Aryans is the Vedas. Today orthodox Hindus—who think of themselves as the heirs of the Aryan people—regard the Vedas as their oldest and most sacred scripture. Most Hindus believe that the Vedas are divine knowledge containing the deep secrets of the universe. They call the Vedas *shruti,* a word that means revelation. According to traditional Hindu belief, the Vedas have no author but were revealed to certain ancient sages by reality itself.

The Vedas are divided into four collections. The oldest of these collections, and the one we'll be concerned with in our study, is the Rig Veda. The Rig Veda contains over a thousand songs to various gods and goddesses. Some scholars have argued that the Rig Veda may be over 30,000 years old, but most believe it to have a far more recent origin, between 2300 and 1200 B.C.E. In any event, the Vedas were clearly pre-Axial. They were also kept in oral tradition for centuries and probably not written down until well after the Axial Age.

What the Vedas tell us is that religion in Indo-Aryan life was principally a matter of ritual and sacrifice. As with the Indus culture, Aryan ritual seems to be very much a this-worldly affair, focused mainly on getting the necessary goods for a happy and comfortable life in the here-and-now. The Vedas were instructions and prayers and hymns created for the purpose of performing these rituals. To gain an understanding of the Vedic worldview, we'll look at some of these rituals and why they were performed and to whom they addressed. And we'll begin with this last question first: who were the gods for whom Vedic ceremonies were enacted?

Tradition says that there are 33 different gods and goddesses in the Vedas, although that's not the exact number. These gods—known in Sanskrit, you'll remember, as *devas*—were believed to dwell on earth, in heaven, and in the mid-space between heaven and earth, a tripartite world not unlike that of the Iranians. Most of the *devas* were understood to have specific functions or realms associated with them. Indra, for instance, was the god of war. He led the Aryans into battle and served as the model soldier. According to Zoroaster, Indra was one of the principal devas associated with chaos and evil. Like other devas, Indra also ruled a province of nature; in this case, the waters of heavens that brought the monsoons.

Agni was the divine fire, who lived on earth in the domestic fireplace, the hearth, and in plants. He also dwelled in mid-space as lightning and in heaven as the fire of the sun. Because of his versatility, Agni was the mediator between gods and humans and therefore figured prominently in the Aryan rituals.

There was also Surya, the god of the sun; Yama, the king of death; Ushas, the goddess of the dawn; Kubera, the deva of wealth and prosperity; and a whole host of lesser divine beings of different ranks and qualities, including the asuras, whom the Indo-Aryans considered evil.

At different stages in Vedic religion, different devas took center stage. Although there were many gods, when the Aryans worshipped, they often treated one god or one goddess as the supreme deity. Generally, the Aryans worshipped that deva whose favors were needed at the moment. As Aryan interests and needs evolved, so did their worship practices. We can discern, for instance, that the war deva Indra was much more important in the early Vedic period than later when the Aryans were more settled and more concerned with agriculture and ranching.

In our next lecture, we will investigate how the Indo-Aryans related to their gods, but before we do let's spend a moment on how these people viewed themselves and their place in the universe. After all, much of what is at stake in the Axial Age is the transformation of human self-understanding.

One of the most telling observations about Vedic views of human nature and destiny is that the Vedas have very little to say on the subject. We find very few statements explicitly addressing this question, and so we must rely on inference. It's apparent that the Aryans didn't spend a lot of time analyzing themselves and developing a systematic self-understanding. This point comes into great relief when we compare the Vedic speculation on human nature to the incredible energy spent on self-scrutiny in the Axial era. The Vedas are by far more interested in the praise of the gods and the performance of sacrifices and other rituals than in attempting to understand what it means to be human. Or maybe it might be more accurate to say that it is through ritual that the Aryans understood the meaning of being human.

One place in the Vedas where we get some sense of the Aryan perspective on the human self is the few hymns in the Rig Veda concerning death. We shouldn't be too surprised to discover Aryan reflections on the essence of being human in this context. In the face of death—whether that of our selves or of others—we humans almost reflexively raise questions about the essential nature of who we are and what our lives mean. When it rises to consciousness, the prospect of death has a profound way of prompting us to think about the real significance of our lives.

In these Vedic hymns we discover fairly wide-ranging speculation about what occurs at death. In one hymn alone, several fates for the human individual are mentioned as possibilities. In one verse, the individual is believed to travel to heaven, carried by the cremation fires, where he or she joins the ancestors and the gods in a relatively pleasant post-mortem existence. In another verse in the same hymn, the individual is seen as dissolving into the elements of the natural world. Addressing the dead person, the hymn says, "May your eye go to the sun, your life's breath to the wind. Go to the sky or to the earth, as is your nature; or go down to the waters, if that is your fate. Take root in the plants with your limbs."

Still later, the same hymn suggests that perhaps the corpse is "cooked," to use its language, by the funeral pyre, to make it a fit sacrifice to be consumed by the gods. Other Vedic hymns suggest that the soul descends to something called the house of clay, the underworld ruled by the god of death Yama. Obviously, the Vedas do not reach agreement about the ultimate destination of human beings.

Furthermore, these hymns give no sense of consensus about the make-up of the human personality or about what determines one's final destiny. Sometimes, the hymns refer to the soul which is often identified with the breath, or to the *manas*, which is a rather vague idea indicating the mind, the heart, or the life-spirit that animates the body. But just as these realities are not well developed as ideas in the Vedas, their relationship to the body is not spelled out.

The Vedas are also not clear about what determines fate. Sometimes it appears as if the correct performance of sacrifices and other rituals is what decides one's destiny: sometimes it seems as if other deeds, like fighting in a battle or giving gifts to the priests, might make this determination. Sometimes it seems as if one's ultimate fate has no relationship at all to how one lived his or her life. One thing is fairly clear though: the Vedas make no unambiguous and certain pronouncements that individual destiny—if there is one—is related to moral choices in the way that Zoroaster linked decision and fate.

The Aryans surely regarded death as an occasion for grief and sadness, because life on earth was valuable and precious and something to be held onto for as long as possible. And yet there's no indication that the death was terrifying to the Aryans. There is no suggestion in the Vedas that life after death—if indeed there was one—might be torturous or unpleasant. We might also observe, anticipating our next lecture, that the Rig Veda says nothing of what comes to be called reincarnation, the notion that the spiritual essence of the person resumes life in a new body an infinite number of times. That conception is an Axial development that receives widespread acceptance as the Vedic tradition evolves into Hinduism.

Up to this point, our examination of the Indo-Aryans has focused on their beliefs: what they thought about the divine world and what they thought about themselves and their ultimate destinies. But this picture of Vedic life is still incomplete because we have not yet

explored the very important matter of ritual. When we take up that topic, we will be investigating the dimension of Aryan religion that brings together the divine and human realms. Our turn to ritual will take us into the very heart of pre-Axial religious life in ancient India and will provide the basis for understanding the dramatic transformations that occur when the Axial Age begins.

Lecture Six
The Start of the Indian Axial Age

Scope:

Central to Aryan life, rituals gave meaning to everything from the creation of the universe to the death of the individual. Vedic rituals ensured the proper functioning of the world. The most important ritual was the *shrauta* rite, in which elaborate ceremonies and special functionaries, the priests of the Brahmin caste, helped an individual gain the favor of the gods for particular benefits. But as the Indo-Aryans spread and settled over northern India, many began to question the value of rituals and the power of the priests. Some Aryans began to worry about their individual fates, and death increasingly became a matter of serious concern. The Upanishads, a collection of texts later included among the Hindu scriptures, were composed to help provide answers to the emerging questions about life, death, and the significance of both. This time period marks the beginnings of classical Hinduism and the start of the Indian Axial Age.

Outline

I. Ritual, the essential means for appealing to the divine, was of vital importance to the Aryans in pre-Axial India. To understand the impulses that led to the reinterpretation of ritual during the Axial period, however, we'll first look at the dynamics of pre-Axial ritual.

- **A.** The Vedas are vague about how the Aryans understood human nature and individual destiny, yet the belief structure supporting their rituals was complex and specific.
- **B.** A passage from the Rig Veda illustrates this complexity in a creation story about Purusha, the primordial sacrificial victim. Purusha was a man with "a thousand heads, a thousand eyes, [and] a thousand feet," whose dismembered body was the origin of all creation in the universe.
- **C.** This story illustrates how sacrifice became the method of renewing creation. But the powers responsible for the well-being of life often needed human assistance—priests.

D. Ritual dismemberment as the basis for creation also implies a relationship between the ritual and the world beyond it. By manipulating certain aspects of the ritual, the priests themselves were controlling aspects of life—making them tantamount to gods. The technical term for this belief is *sympathetic magic*.

E. Finally, the myth of Purusha allows us to understand the caste system. The stratification of priests, producers, warriors, and servants was intended by the gods, a fundamental element in the nature of reality. To challenge the system would be akin to challenging the gods, and the consequences would be dire.

II. The Aryans performed many different rituals and for many different reasons, but the most important may have been the *shrauta* rites, particularly the fire sacrifice.

A. *Shrauta* rituals were more elaborate than others and were performed for different occasions, but ordinarily, they were thought to influence worldly gains, such as breeding more and better cattle, producing "manly" sons, or promoting health and longevity.

B. Only members of the *Brahmin*, or priestly, caste could conduct these rituals, because only they had the skill to do so. Setting up and performing the sacrifice might take several days or weeks.

C. Under Brahmin supervision, workers created a sacred space using precise measurements. Earthen altars contained sacred fires and corresponded to Earth, mid-space, and heaven.

D. The gods were invited to attend, and participants drank *soma* and sacrificed animals, which they cooked and offered to the gods and human participants.

E. The most important aspect of the ritual, however, was the singing of prayers and hymns, using verses from the Vedas, by Brahmin priests. The sacred words had to be correctly uttered or the ritual might be ineffective, perhaps even dangerous.

F. In the early Vedic period, the Aryans believed that the sacrifices persuaded the gods to act on behalf of the one making the sacrifice. Over time, however, the ritual itself was the transformative agent. By manipulating the objects of the sacrifice, and especially by uttering powerful words, the Brahmins came to believe that they themselves were controlling the cosmic powers.

G. Eventually, uttering sacred words during rituals became akin to tapping into the creative power of the sacrifice. The priests regarded themselves as the custodians of this power, called *Brahman*, or "that which makes great."

III. Following the Vedic period (1500–800 B.C.E.), the period of *classical Hinduism* marks the time when the complex traditions of Hinduism began to take shape, coinciding with the advent of the Axial Age in India. During this transitional time, significant changes took place.

A. Despite the rise of classical Hinduism, Vedic traditions were retained. Older Vedic notions and practices were kept intact and, to some extent, reinterpreted. In addition, a set of new ideas and concerns was added to the mix, resulting in what we call Hinduism.

B. But changes did occur, and the most important was the expansion of the Indo-Aryans into the Gangetic plain of northeastern India around 1000 B.C.E., sometimes called the "second urbanization" of India. The Aryans eventually gave up the nomadic life, settling in towns and becoming farmers.

C. These basic sociological changes coordinated with certain developments in Indo-Aryan religion, such as growing doubts about the value of ritual.

1. The middle castes may have resented the power of the Brahmins and their monopoly on ritual performance.
2. But perhaps even more important was an emerging sense that rituals were not all that worthwhile.

D. Further, a collection of writings—the Upanishads—from this period began to reevaluate Vedic practices. One story illustrates a dialogue between a young Brahmin, Nachiketas, and Yama, the King of Death.

1. Through an interesting set of circumstances, Nachiketas is sent to the underworld, where Yama grants him three wishes.

2. For his third wish, Nachiketas asks Yama to explain what happens when a person dies, but Yama is reluctant to answer.
3. As an alternative to answering the question, Yama offers Nachiketas wealth and longevity on Earth, precisely what the Vedic rituals were intended to secure and what the Indo-Aryans may have considered the highest goods of life. Nachiketas refuses these gifts in favor of his desire to know about the afterlife.

E. The story of Nachiketas at the dawn of the Axial Age signifies an important shift among some practitioners of Indian religion: Earthly riches now count for little. It wasn't that practitioners believed the old rituals didn't work but that what the rituals provided was ultimately unimportant.

F. Finally, for the first time in early Indian literature, expressions of anxiety about death appear. In earlier passages from the Rig Veda, there is no agreement about the ultimate fate of human beings and no sense that the Indo-Aryans were even concerned about the afterlife. The stage is now set for change.

Essential Reading:

Hopkins, *The Hindu Religious Tradition*, chapter 2.

Supplementary Reading:

Mascaró, *The Upanishads*, "Katha Upanishad."

Questions to Consider:

1. How did the concept and practice of ritual evolve among the Aryans?
2. What is the significance of the story of Nachiketas and his encounter with Yama?

Lecture Six—Transcript
The Start of the Indian Axial Age

Our first look into the religious environment of ancient India revealed a world of gods and goddesses controlling the various aspects of existence that were of particular concern to the inhabitants of the Indus valley and their Aryan successors. The interest the Aryans and Indus dwellers had in their gods seemed to focus on the ways these powerful beings could help sustain and improve human life on earth. Gods and goddesses might be called upon to render aid in a battle, or stave off disease, or to facilitate reproduction.

The essential means for making these appeals to the divine was ritual. Ritual was of vital importance in pre-Axial India, especially to the Aryans, whose entire scripture was dedicated to its proper practice. For the first part of this talk we will focus on the nature of these ceremonies, attending especially to the beliefs about how they accomplished their intended purpose. It's important to understand the dynamics of pre-Axial ritual in order to grasp the impulses that led to the reevaluation and reinterpretation of ritual in the Axial period. By the time we have finished with this discussion, we will have seen some of the new ideas that have begun to emerge in Indian religion that provided the foundations for Hinduism, Buddhism, and Jainism.

We've already seen that the Aryans did not have a highly developed or consistent self-understanding. The Vedas are rather vague about how the Aryans understood human nature or the ultimate destiny of the individual. But we shouldn't infer from this that they were somehow incapable of sophisticated or systematic thinking. When we come to Vedic ritual practices, it becomes abundantly evident that the Aryans were able to think in complex and abstract ways. In fact, it's rather amazing to observe the intense intellectual energy the Aryans devoted to understanding and practicing their rituals.

To illustrate the complexity of the belief-structure supporting their ritual practices, I'd like to examine an intriguing passage from the Rig Veda that describes the world's creation. This myth is actually one of half-a-dozen creation stories in the Rig Veda alone. The Aryans were obviously not greatly troubled by having several different creation myths.

The passage is a well-known story that describes the ritual dismemberment of a primordial person. This myth is a late addition to the Vedic corpus, which puts it fairly close to the start of the Axial Age. But it clearly echoes a very ancient creation theme: the idea that the world is created by the gods through sacrifice. That theme, you'll remember, was also part of the Avestan cosmogony of Iranian religion.

In the Vedic version, the sacrificial victim is called the Purusha, who is described as a massive cosmic man with a "thousand heads, a thousand eyes, [and] a thousand feet," larger than the physical universe itself. I'll read the relevant parts of the story and then comment on them afterwards.

> When the gods spread the sacrifice with the Man as the offering, spring was the clarified butter, summer the fuel, and autumn the oblation.
>
> They anointed the Man, the sacrifice born at the beginning, upon the sacred grass. With him the gods…sacrificed.
>
> From that sacrifice in which everything was offered, the melted fat was collected, and he made it into those beasts who live in the air, in the forest, and in the villages.
>
> From that sacrifice in which everything was offered, the verses and chants were born, the metres were born from it, and from it the formulas were born. [The passage is actually saying that the Vedas themselves—including this very story that I'm reading—come from this sacrifice.]
>
> Horses were born from it, and those other animals that have two rows of teeth; cows were born from it, and from it goats and sheep were born.
>
> When they divided the Man, into how many parts did they apportion him? What do they call his mouth, his two arms, his thighs and his feet?
>
> His mouth became the [Priest]; his arms were made into the Warrior, his thighs the [Producers], and from his feet the servants were born.
>
> The moon was born from his mind; from his eye the sun was born. Indra and Agni came from his mouth, and from his vital breath the Wind was born.

> From his navel realm the middle space arose; from his head the sky evolved. From his two feet came the earth, and the quarters of the sky from his ear. Thus they set the worlds in order.

One important thing about this hymn is the way it established reciprocal relationships among the sacrifice, the act of creation, and the elements of the world. Because the sacrifice was the primordial mode of creation, sacrifice now became the method by which to renew creation, to recreate and maintain the world periodically when it became necessary. Performing sacrifice, like the gods did at the beginning of time, renewed and invigorated the world. The priests who thus performed sacrifices—and this was clearly the way the Aryans understood it—were reenacting creation itself, making them tantamount to gods.

It may be difficult for those of us in the modern world to completely grasp this ancient need to participate in the process of cosmic regeneration. We moderns think that the world proceeds on its own. We don't perform ceremonies to help the sun come up in the morning or to ensure the change of seasons is regular and timely. We don't coax seeds to sprout and produce abundant crops with rituals. But the ancient world often viewed the human relationship to the natural world quite differently. For many ancients, the powers responsible for the well being of life often needed human assistance. In the Iranian tradition, we noted this belief in the practice of pouring libations of milk into water or animal fat into the fire. The human and divine worlds maintained a symbiotic relationship. Each relied on the other for the maintenance of life.

The formation of the parts of the world out of the ritual dismemberment of the first man also implies a system of relationships between the ritual and the greater world beyond it. If, as the story suggests, the seasons are identified with the components of the sacrifice (and that is the meaning of that very cryptic phrase, "spring was the clarified butter, summer the fuel, and autumn the oblation"), then by manipulating these aspects of the ritual, the priests were effectively controlling the seasons themselves. The technical term for this belief is sympathetic magic.

Sir James Frazer, one of the early theorists on magic and religion and the author of an influential book entitled *The Golden Bough*, explained it this way: "things having been in contact with each other continue to react upon one another at a distance even after they have been severed or disconnected." Because everything was once connected to the Purusha and because the Purusha is sympathetically connected to the ritual, the performance of ritual sacrifice was understood to have effects in the world beyond. You might liken this manner of thinking to the way voodoo dolls are supposed to affect the person they represent. Thus, a pin stuck in the doll is believed to cause pain to the one it symbolized.

Finally, the myth of the Purusha has implications for the understanding of caste, which is mentioned here for the first time in the Vedas. In previous discussions we've witnessed the gradual evolution of the caste system among the Aryans, beginning with the simple distinction of priests and producers among the earliest Indo-Aryans. Then we saw the addition of the warrior caste as the cattle rustling and village raiding life became more popular, creating a three-tiered society of priests, warriors, and the producers—the ones in charge of raising crops and tending livestock. The fourth and lowest tier in the Aryan system was probably made up of the indigenous people from the old Indus culture.

The story of the Purusha obviously suggests that the stratification of humanity into priests, warriors, producers, and servants is both intended by the gods and embedded in the very fabric of the cosmos. This account of the divine origin of caste is part of the ideological structure that has kept this system in place for over 3,000 years. In other words, caste is not regarded as a mere social construction, but as a fundamental element in the nature of reality. To attempt to challenge the system would be like challenging the gods or gravity, and the consequences would be dire.

These principles were the basis for the Aryans' understanding of the necessity of ritual and its effectiveness. As we might expect, the Aryans performed many different kinds of rituals and for many different reasons. Like many ancient cultures—and many societies still today—Vedic rituals prescribed ceremonies to assist individuals during times of crisis (such as sickness); or through times of transition (such as birth, marriage, or death); or on auspicious days (such as the new moon or harvest time). Rituals also provided protection from demons and snakes, and promoted good luck in gambling, and caused misfortune to one's enemies.

But the most important sacrifices for Aryan religious life may have been the *shrauta* rites, particularly the fire sacrifice. *Shrauta* rituals were more elaborate than the other rituals and were performed with less frequency. *Shrauta* rites were conducted for different occasions, such as a coronation. Wealthy people could also pay to have the rites performed on their behalf. Only members of the Brahmin, or priestly caste, were able to enact these kinds of rituals. The *shrauta* ritual required great skill, and only those with the training of a Brahmin had the requisite expertise. Indeed, as these rituals grew in importance for the Aryans, the Brahmins grew in power and prestige.

A typical *shrauta* sacrifice involved a team of Brahmins, each charged with different responsibilities: setting up and performing the sacrifice might take several days or even weeks. Under Brahmin supervision, workers created a sacred space outdoors by erecting a temporary canopy using very precise measurements. Under the canopy, earthen altars were created to contain the sacred fires. Three altars each corresponded to a component of the world: the earth, midspace, and heaven. Once the ritual was underway, the gods were invited to attend. *Soma*—that divine beverage prized by the Indo-Iranians—was drunk and an animal, such as a goat, was sacrificed and cooked: and then the sacred food was offered to the gods and human participants.

The most important aspect of the sacrifice, however, were the hymns and prayers sung by the Brahmin priests. These verses were taken from the Vedas, and it was essential that they be chanted correctly. One priest's sole responsibility was to be sure that the sacred words were accurately uttered. He corrected any mistakes made by the others. Mistakes rendered the ritual ineffective, and perhaps even dangerous; and hence, the Brahmins placed great importance on the exact memorization of the Veda.

Shrauta rituals were performed for a variety of reasons, but ordinarily they had this-worldly aims. Sacrificers—that is, the ones who paid for the ceremony—sought to improve their relations with the gods in order to achieve greater success in business, to breed more and better cattle, to produce what the Veda calls "manly" sons, and to promote health and longevity. The attainment of a pleasant afterlife in heaven might also be added to this list, but that goal seems to be secondary to the others.

In the early Vedic period, the Aryans believed that the sacrifices persuaded the gods to act on behalf of the sacrificer. Persuasion came in the form of flattering songs sung in honor of a deva and the offering of delicious food to eat and Soma to drink. But over time the ritual itself came to be regarded as the transformative agent. Priests no longer thought of themselves as urging the gods to act in certain ways. By manipulating the objects of the sacrifice and especially by uttering powerful words they called mantras, the Brahmins came to believe that they themselves were controlling the cosmic powers. Now, this belief seems to be the logical development of the idea of corresponding relationships between the ritual and the world.

Eventually, the sacred words used during rituals came to be seen as powerful in themselves. The utterance of these words generated or tapped into the creative power of the sacrifice. The priests called this power *Brahman*, a word that means "that which makes great," and they came to regard themselves as the custodians of this Brahman.

Now let's take a moment to summarize some of the key points about Vedic ritual. First, ritual is immensely important in Vedic religion. The Aryans, like most pre-Axial peoples, were not terribly anxious about belief and doctrine. But they were greatly interested in the correct performance of specific religious acts because these ceremonies and sacrifices were integral to their well being on earth and maybe even to their destiny after death.

Gradually, these ritual practices came to be regarded as the special province of experts, individuals trained to enact these ceremonies in precise ways. As these religious practices were developed and refined, the Indo-Aryans came to believe that the rituals themselves were powerful. It was not so much that the rites persuaded or prompted the gods to act on human behalf: rather, the rite itself—and especially the words of the ritual—came to be seen as the true agent of control.

This brief summary fairly accurately characterizes the world of Indo-Aryan religion near the end of what we conventionally call the Vedic period of Indian religious history, roughly the time between 1500 and 800 B.C.E. This era is succeeded by what is known as classical Hinduism, so designated because during this time the complex of traditions that we refer to as Hinduism begins to take its characteristic shape. The rise of classical Hinduism also coincides with the advent of the Axial Age in India. So it will be important for us to spend some time examining this transitional moment, to grasp the factors that mark the close of the Vedic era and the opening of classical Hinduism.

When I say the Vedic period closed and the classical Hindu period began, I do not mean to imply that one era superseded the other. The rise of classical Hinduism did not mean that Vedic religion was no longer practiced or that it gradually faded into oblivion. To the contrary, the Vedic traditions were retained and still performed. Perhaps a better way of imagining this development is to think that as classical Hinduism arises, Indian religion enlarges. The older Vedic notions and practices are kept intact and, to some extent, they are reinterpreted. In addition, a new set of ideas and concerns are added to this mix and the resulting amalgam is what we call Hinduism. Perhaps the situation is not so different from the way Christianity developed out of Judaism; retaining many of the Jewish elements, reinterpreting others, and then adding novel features from other sources. The appearance of classical Hinduism, therefore, does not mean the disappearance of Indo-Aryan religion.

But changes did occur, and the changes were motivated by a number of factors, many of which seem to be characteristic of Axial changes throughout the world. One of the most important of these is the expansion of the Indo-Aryans into the Gangetic plain of northeastern India, beginning around 1000 B.C.E. This extension of Aryan culture entailed what some call the second urbanization of India. The Aryans began to give up the nomadic life, settle in villages and towns, and became farmers. This development eventually led to a period of greater material progress and put the Indo-Aryans in greater contact with non-Aryan peoples.

These basic sociological changes were coordinated with certain developments in Indo-Aryan religion. For instance, late in the Vedic period, there seem to be growing doubts about the value of ritual. In part, these questions about ritual seem to be associated with the resentment of the middle castes to the power of the Brahmin priests and their monopoly on ritual performance. But perhaps even deeper than that was the emerging sense that what the rituals accomplished was not, in the final analysis, all that worthwhile.

We see these doubts arising from a collection of writings from near the time of the end of the Vedic period and the start of classical

Hinduism. This collection, which we'll discuss in much greater detail later, is known as the Upanishads. For now I simply want to excerpt a passage to illustrate the point I'm making about the reevaluation of Vedic practices. This particular selection is a dialogue between a young Brahmin and Yama, the God of Death. Through an interesting set of circumstances, this young man—whose name is Nachiketas—finds himself sent to the underworld, where he is forced to wait for three days without food because the King of Death is away, doing what it is that the grim reaper does. When Yama returns home to the underworld, he realizes he has committed a great offense by neglecting his obligations of hospitality to a Brahmin. To atone for his mistake, Yama offers to grant Nachiketas three wishes.

For his third and most important wish, Nachiketas asks Yama to explain to him what happens when a persons dies, a seemingly simple request to make of the god of death—or so one would think. Yama is surprisingly reluctant to answer this simple question. The dialogue proceeds in this manner:

> Nachiketas says: When a man dies, this doubt arises: some say 'he is' and some say 'he is not.'
>
> And Death responds: Even the gods had this doubt in times of old; for mysterious is the law of life and death. Ask for another boon. Release me from this.
>
> Nachiketas: This doubt indeed arose even to the gods, and you say, O Death, that it is difficult to understand; but no greater teacher than you can explain it, and there is no other boon as great as this.
>
> Death says: Take horses and gold and cattle and elephants; choose sons and grandsons that shall live a hundred years. Have vast expanses of land, and live as many years as you desire. Or choose another gift that you think equal to this, and enjoy it with wealth and long life. Be a ruler of this vast earth. I will grant you all your desires. Ask for any wishes, however hard to obtain…. and I will give you fair maidens with chariots and musical instruments. But ask me not, Nachiketas, the secrets of death.
>
> Nachiketas responds: All these pleasures pass away, O End of all! They weaken the power of life. And indeed how short

> is all life! Keep your horses and dancing and singing. Man cannot be satisfied with wealth. Shall we enjoy wealth with you in sight? Shall we live while you are in power? I can only ask for the boon I have asked.... Solve then the doubt as to the great beyond. Grant me the gift that unveils the mystery.

This brief passage is important to our study for a number of reasons. I'll begin with what may not be so obvious on a causal reading, and that is what Yama offers Nachiketas as alternatives to having to answer the question about the afterlife. The king of death promises the young Brahmin cattle and horses; wealth, power, and land; and children and a long comfortable life. What is significant to observe is that these all are things that are precisely what the Vedic rituals were intended to secure. In an earlier age, the Indo-Aryans may have considered these things the highest goods of life. What more could one hope for? Wealth, children, long life—these were the epitome of the good life.

And yet now, in this passage from the dawn of the Axial Age, those things count for little. An important shift has occurred—or has begun to occur—among some practitioners of Indian religion. What was seen as most valuable in life is now regarded with significantly less favor, and perhaps even with a touch of contempt. As Nachiketas says, these things "weaken the power of life." There is an implicit criticism of Vedic ritual that should not be missed here. It's not so much that later thinkers were suggesting that the old rituals did not work; rather, they were saying that what the rituals provide is ultimately not so important.

A second point is also significant. For the first time in the early Indian literature, we have begun to hear expressions of anxiety about death. Nachiketas wants to know: after death, does the individual exist or not? There is an urgency and an intensity in his question. He wants to know the answer and he refuses to let the god of death off the hook. There's nothing like this in the earlier Vedic literature. Previously, we looked at some of the passages about death from the old Rig Veda, and we noted a good deal of speculation but the lack of any agreement about the ultimate human fate. What we did not encounter was the sense that the afterlife was a pressing issue of concern for the Indo-Aryans. If they gave it much thought at all, some of the Aryans believed that death conferred a pleasant existence in heaven with the ancestors; or others imagined a kind of dissolution of the soul and body as they melted into their elemental forms; and some may have thought that the corpse was consumed by the gods. What seemed to be lacking was the sense that knowing what lay on the other side of death was a matter of deep concern.

The stage is now set for change. In the next chapter of Indian religious history, questions that are now appearing here and there—questions about the ultimate destiny of human beings, about the nature of existence after death, and the absolute reality of the entire cosmos—these questions will take center stage. And a whole new cast of characters will appear to address them.

Lecture Seven
Death and Rebirth

Scope:

A key element in the evolution of Hinduism was the widespread acceptance of the concept of *samsara*, the belief that beings endure a beginningless series of births, deaths, and rebirths, governed by the moral principle known as *karma*. This lecture explores the development of these major concepts and the novel problems they presented to Indian religion and philosophy. Once these ideas were accepted, virtually every school of philosophy or sect of religion that arose in India's history—including Buddhism and Jainism—took *samsara* as the fundamental predicament of existence, and each in its own way sought to address this problem. This new religious problematic signaled India's entrance into the Axial Age.

Outline

I. Between 800–600 B.C.E., Indian religious life began to change dramatically. The old Vedic ritual system, which had dominated Aryan religion for centuries, came under scrutiny, and material earthly riches became less important than spiritual gains.

A. As people became more prosperous, sages began to wonder if there were more to life—if human existence could transcend the acquisition of material success.

B. There was an increasing concern with death and the ultimate fate of individuals, a departure from the Vedic focus on the complete enjoyment of earthly life.

C. For certain groups of Aryans, probably Brahmins and others acquainted with the Vedas, the question of death and afterlife was a matter of much discussion and speculation, though opinions were diverse and inconsistent.

D. Doubts began to arise about the Vedic picture of the afterlife, in which one enjoyed a pleasant and permanent existence among the gods and ancestors. Although this was not a universal Aryan view, many believed it and thought that performing the appropriate rituals was the way to secure it.

II. At the end of the Vedic era and the start of the Axial Age, the fear arose that one might initially reach heaven only to lose it again through death. The word *redeath* now entered the religious lexicon, implying that one died, ascended to heaven for a time, then died again, dissolving into the elements of the natural world.

A. The notion of redeath was probably an intermediate step toward the concept of reincarnation, or transmigration of the soul, where one endures a continual series of births, deaths, and rebirths.

B. No one is sure how belief in reincarnation appeared and became widely accepted throughout India, but it likely began in northern India among a small coterie of philosophers and holy persons at the start of the Axial Age.

C. Not unique to India, the concept of reincarnation is found among some Native Americans, the Trobriand Islanders, and in West Africa. The idea was also popular with Pythagoras, Socrates, and other Axial Age philosophers of ancient Greece—descendants of the Indo-Europeans.

D. Rebirth became the fundamental assumption of virtually all Indian religions and philosophies, including Hinduism, Buddhism, and Jainism. Though these religions interpret rebirth in different ways, the common term used to denote this concept is *samsara*, or "wandering."

III. The ancient Indian Upanishads give us the first clear sense of reincarnation. But before we delve deeper into that topic, let's look more closely at this classic text, because it is vital to understanding subsequent developments in Indian religion.

A. The most important Upanishads were probably composed between 800–400 B.C.E., squarely in the Axial Age. The number of Upanishads varies, but most editions contain 13 or 14 "principal" Upanishads.

B. By tradition, the Upanishads are considered part of the Vedas and, like the Vedas, are not systematic or always consistent. But the Upanishads represent a different view of the world from the earlier Vedic texts, such as the Rig Veda.

C. Whereas the earlier Vedas are centrally concerned with rituals and sacrifice, the Upanishads are much more contemplative. They seem to reflect the outlook of the solitary ascetic or seeker, rather than the world of the priest or religious official.

D. Despite the clear differences with earlier Vedic texts, the Upanishads are still regarded as *śruti*—revealed knowledge—sharing the same sacred status as the Vedas.

E. Like the Old and New Testaments, the Upanishads and the Vedas were written during different epochs. As with the New Testament, the Upanishads more clearly and completely describe revelations than the Vedas (or Old Testament); this explains the apparent inconsistencies and tensions between the two works. Thus, the Upanishads are often called *Vedanta*, which means the "completion of the Veda."

F. Written earlier, the Vedas make no mention of the concept of transmigration, but by the time the Upanishads appear, the concept of rebirth has started to enjoy widespread acceptance. Yet the Upanishadic passages deal with rebirth through metaphor or analogy, rather then clearly spelling out what it is.

G. Some passages imply that reincarnation is driven by one's desire to be reborn. Other views hypothesize that cremation fires convert corpses into smoke, which carries the dead to heaven; there, they become food for the gods, before returning to Earth through a series of natural events and being reborn in male semen.

IV. As the Axial Age progresses and the Upanishads develop further, the details of reincarnation are refined. One of the most important of these developments is the concept of *karma*. Whereas the idea of rebirth is not exclusive to India, the belief that one's future incarnation depends on how one behaves in this life *is* a distinctive Indian contribution.

A. In older Vedic times, karma referred to ritual action that priests performed to make a sacrifice effective. But in the development of classical Hinduism, karma came to include the idea of moral action. Like Zoroaster's beliefs, the Upanishads make one's moral behavior the decisive element in human destiny.

B. Karma is a theory that states that the events in one's life—good or bad—are neither chance occurrences nor foreordained by realities outside of oneself. Rather, the concept refers to one's actions and their consequences.

C. Karma does not separate action from consequences; the effects of one's acts will eventually return to the actor in what is known as the *fruiting of karma.*

D. Karma is inevitable, always returning to the agent who created it, no matter how long it takes, even more than one lifetime.

E. Karma pertains not only to physical acts but to thoughts and words, indicating a growing focus during this time on the interiority of the spiritual life, a characteristic of Axial transformations throughout the world.

F. Karma can be good or evil, positive or negative. In essence, by performing good actions, one produces positive karma; wicked or irresponsible actions create negative karma.

G. Karma is a principle of absolute justice, a process that occurs ineluctably and impersonally, with no god or divine being meting out justice. According to Hinduism, even the gods themselves are subject to karma.

Essential Reading:

Sharma, *Classical Hindu Thought*, chapters 11–13.

Supplementary Reading:

Obeyesekere, *Imagining Karma,* chapter 1.

Questions to Consider:

1. The idea of *samsara* may have developed independently of the concept of karma. Is it possible to believe in karma without holding to the notion of rebirth?
2. Does it take more faith to believe in reincarnation than to believe in the annihilation of the self at death or in the resurrection of the dead?

3. What would it take to persuade you to accept the principle of karma?

Lecture Seven—Transcript
Death and Rebirth

At the end of our last talk, we found ourselves in the midst of a transition in Indian religious history. We had begun to observe the close of the Vedic age and the advent of the era of classical Hinduism, a period that coincides with the Axial era. Of course, there's no distinct moment in time when we can say definitively that the Vedic period has ended and the classical period has begun. As I mentioned previously, the Vedic traditions were largely retained and embraced by the emerging Hinduism. What distinguishes the classical Hindu era is the reorientation of religious life to new concerns and new beliefs. This evolution took place over a 200-year span, beginning around 800 B.C.E. and continuing on to about the year 600 B.C.E., at least according to western ways of reckoning time.

During these 200 years, Indian religious life began to change dramatically. The venerable old Vedic ritual system, which had dominated Aryan religion for centuries, came under scrutiny. Increasingly, some thinkers expressed doubts about the kinds of benefits the Vedic rituals could produce. It was not so much that the Indo-Aryans no longer valued long life, health, material prosperity, and children—the sorts of things rituals were intended to accomplish: rather, these items of the good life had now begun to be regarded as less important in the grand scheme of things. Sages were starting to wonder: Is this all there is to life, or does human existence have some meaning, some significance that transcends the acquisition of these things, as good and as valuable as they are?

This question began to arise with more frequency as the Aryans began to enjoy greater material success as they settled in villages and became agriculturists. As concerns with subsistence needs receded into the background, other questions—what we might call philosophical or transcendental issues—seem to have come to the fore. The increase in material well-being does not wholly account for this philosophical turn, but surely it played a part. How many of us—particularly in our affluent society—after having attained everything we thought we wanted, raised our heads and asked, Is this all?

I'll never forget the experience of watching my five-year-old nephew open a couple of dozen Christmas gifts one year and when they had all been unwrapped, he looked at his parents and said, "Is this all?" For a variety of reasons, growing numbers of individuals throughout Northern India at the time we're considering were asking the same question: Is this all there is? Is there something more to life than simply satisfying our desires, and if so, how do we find it?

Closely connected with these questions was an increasing concern with death and the ultimate fate of the individual person. The Indo-Aryans of the Vedic period were not unconcerned about death, but their interest was not a great preoccupation or a matter of great passion. The face of death was neither terrifying nor the object of intense speculation. Death was a simple reality of life, and the point of existence seemed to be to enjoy what the world had to offer before death comes. There was nothing in Vedic culture to suggest anything like what Ernst Becker called the denial of death. To be sure, some passages in the Vedas intimated that there may be some form of existence beyond the personal demise of the individual, but this was by no means a consistent or universal belief. The clear emphasis throughout the Vedas was on the complete enjoyment of the goods of the earthly life.

But as the Axial Age comes into full manifestation, the issue of death becomes a topic of greater attention, and it's approached with an unprecedented energy. In our last lecture, we saw this exemplified in the tale of Nachiketas and his dialogue with Yama, the king of death. Rather than accept the pleasures of the earthly life, the young Brahmin compelled the god of the underworld to reveal to him the secrets of existence beyond death, a demand that Yama was extremely reluctant to grant.

As Nachiketas's dialogue with the king of death demonstrates, the question of death and afterlife was a matter of much discussion and speculation among certain groups of Aryans. Most of these were likely to be the Brahmins and other caste members acquainted with the Vedas and sufficiently leisured to ponder these kinds of questions. At any rate, the evidence that remains comes only from these educated classes, and it suggests that conjectures about death were very diverse and anything but consistent.

Among the many ideas being tossed about among philosophically minded individuals, one is of particular interest for subsequent Hindu thinking. We noted in looking at the Rigveda that some Aryans understood death as the transition of the body or the life-force to heaven, where the individual enjoyed a pleasant and permanent existence among the gods and ancestors. One of the Vedic hymns promoting this view encourages believers with this promise: "this pasture…shall not be taken away." Although this was by no means a universal Aryan view, certainly a significant number believed it and many thought that performing the appropriate sacrifices and rituals was the way to secure it.

Yet now, at the end of the Vedic era and the start of the Axial Age, doubts began to creep into this picture of the afterlife. Some of the later portions of the Vedas express suspicions about the permanency of existence in heaven once it has been attained. In these later texts, the fear arises that one might initially reach the heavenly goal only to lose it again through death. The word *redeath* now enters the religious lexicon to describe a situation in which the individual dies and ascends to heaven, then lives there for a time, and then dies again, this time dissolving into the elements of the natural world. Now, it doesn't take much imagination to see how this emerging notion of destiny is beginning to take on some rather ominous qualities. I don't know about you, but I think *one* death will be plenty for me: the idea I might have to endure *more* is pretty distressing!

The notion of redeath was probably an intermediate step towards the development of the concept of reincarnation, or what is known more technically as the transmigration of the soul. This idea—that the individual self endures a continual series of births, deaths, and rebirths—seems to have appeared for the first time in India at the start of the Axial Age. Some have suggested that perhaps the idea of rebirth developed initially within the old Indus culture, and then later reappeared after a period of suppression by the Aryans. But there's really no evidence to support that conjecture.

The truth is that we aren't altogether sure how the belief in reincarnation appeared and then became widely accepted throughout India. The concept of rebirth is certainly not unique to India. We find the notion among some Native Americans, and the Trobriand Islanders, and even in West Africa. And perhaps most significantly for our study is that we find the idea of rebirth among Pythagoras, Socrates, and some of the other Axial Age philosophers of ancient Greece, who were descendants of the Indo-Europeans. By the way, if you're interested in the Greek conception of the afterlife, please take a look at Plato's *Phaedo*, which narrates the story of Socrates' last day of life.

My own belief, which is shared by other scholars of ancient religious life in India, is that the concept of rebirth begins in Northern India among a small coterie of philosophers and holy persons, just as it did in Greece. These Indian thinkers taught this idea to growing numbers of ordinary folk, and eventually it was widely accepted. Interestingly, in ancient Greece the idea of rebirth always remained a philosopher's notion and never caught on with the masses of people.

But in India, the idea of rebirth was so extensively accepted that it became the fundamental assumption of virtually all religions and philosophies, including Hinduism, Buddhism, and Jainism. Each of these traditions understand rebirth in different ways, but the basic sense that existence is characterized by an endless series of births, deaths, and rebirths is common to them all. The term used by these traditions to denote this situation is *samsara*, a word that literally means wandering, suggesting a kind of aimlessness or pointlessness to the process.

The first place in the ancient Indian texts where we get a clear sense of the idea of transmigration is a collection of writings I mentioned earlier: the Upanishads. Before we delve deeper into the topic of rebirth, let me take just a few moments to say more about this classic text since it so vital to understanding subsequent developments in Indian religion.

The most important Upanishads were probably composed between 800 and 400 B.C.E., and that, of course, places them right squarely in the Axial Age. The authors of these works—and there were many of them—are not known today who they were. Clearly they were individuals of a philosophical mindset, seeking answers to the fundamental mysteries of life. There's no universal agreement about what works are contained in this collection. According to some, there are as many as 200–300 Upanishads. A more commonly given number is 108, which is a particularly sacred number in Hinduism and Buddhism. Most editions and English translations contain 13 or 14 so-called Principal Upanishads. Because they are rooted in the Axial period, these Principal Upanishads will be the source for our discussion.

By tradition, the Upanishads are considered part of the Vedas. Like the earlier Vedas, the Upanishads are not systematic or always internally consistent. But a careful reading of the Upanishads clearly reveals that they represent a very different view of the world from the earlier Vedic texts like the Rig Veda. Whereas the earlier Vedas are centrally concerned with rituals and sacrifice, the Upanishads are much more contemplative and thoughtful in tone. They seem to reflect the outlook of the solitary ascetic, or seeker, rather than the world of the priest or the religious official.

Despite the clear differences with the earlier Vedic texts and the Upanishads, the Upanishads are still regarded as *śruti*, or revealed knowledge, which means they share the same sacred status as the earlier Vedas. The Upanishads are often called *Vedanta*, which means the end and completion of the Veda. The word Vedanta is also the name for a particular school of Hindu philosophy based on the Upanishads, but for the purposes of discussing Axial Age religions, I'll use the term to refer to the Upanishadic outlook itself, to remind us of its continuity with—and its difference—from the Vedas.

We might compare the relationship of the Upanishads to the earlier Vedas to the relationship between the Old and New Testaments, as Christians typically understand it. The Old and New Testaments were written in different epochs in history and, to a careful reader, there are obvious differences in the tenor and theology of the two texts. The traditional Christian explanation of this difference has been to say that both testaments are authentic revelations, but that the New Testament reveals more clearly and completely what was less clearly indicated in the Old Testament. In a similar manner, the Upanishads were later regarded as the completion of the Vedas, both to assert continuity with the older Vedas and to recognize and explain the apparent inconsistencies and tensions between them.

Now, one area where we can easily observe a tension between the older Vedas and the Upanishads is the question of transmigration. It is evident that the earlier Vedas make no mention of such an idea. But by the time the Upanishads appear, the concept of rebirth has started to enjoy a widespread acceptance. Even so, we won't find a clear or systematic understanding of the nature of this process in these writings. Most of the Upanishadic passages dealing with rebirth do so by means of metaphor or analogy. Here is a typical and well-known selection from one of the Upanishads often called "The Supreme Teaching," one of the oldest texts in the collection:

> [Rebirth] is like this. As a caterpillar, when it comes to the tip of a blade of grass, reaches out to a new foothold and draws itself onto it, so the self, after it has knocked down this body and rendered it unconscious, reaches out to a new foothold and draws itself onto it.
>
> [Rebirth] is like this. As a weaver, after she has removed the coloured yarn weaves a different design that is newer and more attractive, so the self, after it has knocked down this body and rendered it unconscious, makes for himself a different figure that is newer and more attractive—the figure of a forefather,…or of a god,…or else the figure of some other being.

These excerpts imply that continued existence is driven by desire; that is, the self that is reincarnated wills to be reborn. And indeed, as we'll see in the later development of Indian theology, desire for life is precisely what propels the process.

But this view of reincarnation was not universally accepted among the sages composing the Upanishads. Another passage from another earlier Upanishad offers a different perspective. And here the author hypothesizes that the cremation fires convert corpses into smoke, which carries them to heaven on the wind, and thereafter other transformations begin to occur, and they became food for the gods. I'm quoting this passage now:

> Then they return by the same path they went—first to space, and from space to the wind. And after the wind has formed, it turns into smoke; after the smoke has formed, it turns into a thunder-cloud; after the thunder-cloud has formed, it turns into a rain-cloud; and after a rain-cloud has formed, it turns into rain, and rains down. On earth they spring up as rice and barley, plants and trees, sesame and beans…. when someone eats that food and deposits the semen, from him one comes into being again.

Apparently, this reincarnation theory is a further development of the old Vedic view that the corpse is cooked and consumed by the gods. And it simply follows that process to its logical end, based on the ancient belief that the male semen actually contains the complete incipient human and the female womb serves as a kind of incubator but doesn't contribute materially to the embryo. I think this is quite an ingenious theory. I'm impressed by how this effort to explain rebirth is, in its own way, quite empirical, by which I mean it reasons inductively from observable phenomena. But for the record, I don't believe that this is how it works!

The point I want to make with both selections is that although the idea of rebirth gained wide acceptance during this period of Indian history, there was no consensus about how it worked or what it actually meant. For instance, it's not even clear what these sages believed was reincarnated or what determined the form of one's next life. One of the passages I quoted suggested that one gets a newer and more attractive body—such as that of a god—but the later Hindu tradition will come to believe that rebirth does not always imply progress or improvement. In fact, rebirth might very well mean going from being a human to being a dog or an insect.

As the Axial Age progresses, and as the Upanishads developed further, many of these issues are addressed and refined. One of the most important of these developments is the idea of *karma*. Karma adds a unique and quite unusual dimension to the Indian view of rebirth. Whereas the idea of rebirth is not exclusive to India, the belief that one's future incarnation depends on how one behaves in this life *is* a distinctive Indian contribution.

The ethicization of rebirth is what the doctrine of karma is all about. Like Zoroaster and the religions influenced by him, the Upanishads make one's moral behavior the decisive element in human destiny. Of course, the Upanishads imagine that destiny in starkly different terms from the West Asian traditions, but the fundamental principle is the same. In the Upanishads—as for the Indian religions generally—karma determines the form and status of one's next birth.

Karma is one of those terms that most westerners are familiar with, but I suspect most who use the term aren't completely sure about its meaning. I often hear people use karma as another word for luck. I've heard people say on more than one occasion, "Well, I guess that's just my bad karma," to explain an unfortunate situation. But karma is not luck, if luck is understood as some kind of random or chance occurrence, nor is it technically understood to be fate, if fate is a preordained sequence of events determined by a god or a superhuman power. In fact, karma means just the opposite of luck and fate in these senses. According to the theory of karma, the events in one's life—good or bad—are not chance occurrences, nor are they foreordained by realities outside of oneself.

Actually, karma is quite easy to understand. Basically, it refers to the actions that one performs and the consequences of those actions. Just as dropping a pebble into a pond causes ripples that reverberate on the surface of the water, so our every action has reverberating consequences. And there's no way to strictly separate action and consequences: the effects of one's act can be considered as part of the act itself, according to Indian thought. The doctrine of karma maintains that those effects will at some point return to the agent, to the one who performed the act in the first place. So the waves created by a dropped pebble reach the edge of the pond and then continue to reverberate back to the point where the pebble was dropped. The return of the consequences of action to the actor is called the *fruiting of karma*.

I think this is what John Lennon was referring to in his song "Instant Karma." The first line of that song is "Instant karma's gonna get you." Well, karma isn't usually or even always instant, but it is certainly inevitable, and it always returns to the agent who created it, no matter how long it takes. We sometime experience the consequences of our actions soon after they are committed. An angry person might fairly quickly reap the fruit of her anger as other people act out of anger towards her. Or it may take another lifetime or two for karma to come to fruition. But on this you can be sure: karma *is* going to get you. However, it is important to remember that you are the one who generated the karma in the first place.

Karma is actually a concept that pre-dates the Axial Age, but in Axial India it came to assume a different meaning than before. In older Vedic times, karma referred to ritual action; it was the work that the priests performed to make the sacrifice effective. But in the development of classical Hinduism, it came to include the idea of moral action. Furthermore, moral action came to include not just deeds performed by the body, but also thoughts and words. So with the idea of karma we see both the ethicization of ritual, as well as a growing focus on the interiority of the spiritual life—both characteristics of Axial transformations throughout the world.

The acquisition of these moral dimensions suggests that karma could be of two kinds: good or evil, positive or negative. Actually, the philosophical literature on the kinds of karma is quite complex, so I'm reducing the idea to its elemental forms. But in essence, we can say that by performing good actions, one produces positive karma: wicked, immoral, irresponsible actions create negative karma. And at some point, whether in this life or another, the karma we have generated returns to us: to our benefit, if we are good; and to our detriment, if we are evil.

In short, the concept of karma means that every person gets what he or she deserves. Karma is a principle of absolute justice. This process occurs ineluctably and impersonally, like the law of gravity acting on physical bodies. There's no god or divine being meting out justice. It just happens to be the way the world works. In fact, according to Hinduism, even the gods themselves are subject to the law of karma. What Hindus mean by karma is reflected in the western expression, "what goes around comes around." For better or worse, we cannot escape the consequences of our actions.

We have seen now that Axial Age speculation in ancient India has brought about an important new constellation of ideas: that the individual is consigned to an endless series of births, deaths, and rebirths, governed by moral deeds. As this notion is worked out in greater detail, it gains wide acceptance throughout the Indian populace. But it also generates new problems for the way Indians think about life. The older Vedic beliefs in maximizing the pleasures and comforts of the earthly existence are fading away and new concerns are arising about how to face the world of *samsara*. In our next discussion, we'll begin to explore the quests for answers.

Lecture Eight
The Quest for Liberation

Scope:

India may be the most intensely religious place on Earth, and nowhere is that intensity more evident than in the Axial Age movement that led Indian men and women by the hundreds to renounce the material world and their lives in society to seek the final liberation from samsaric existence. Virtually constituting a fifth caste, ascetics, wandering hermits, teachers, yogis, and holy persons of every stripe left the ordinary life in search of the knowledge that would bring them eternal repose from the endless wheel of rebirth. The search for this knowledge took a wide variety of forms and expressions, giving rise to some of the characteristic religious practices often associated with Hinduism. The historical roots of Buddhism and Jainism can also be traced back to this movement.

Outline

I. The ideas of rebirth and karma may have arisen independently of each other, but if so, they came to be inextricably linked in the Indian imagination during the Axial Age, spawning a new attitude toward life and the world. Karma meant that one's current condition was shaped by the deeds one had performed in the past, creating a level of hierarchy in the present.

- **A.** One might be reborn at any level on this hierarchy, ranging from plant life, to various levels of animal life, to the human realm (and its several castes), and then, to various levels of divinity.
- **B.** Too much bad karma could take one from human existence to that of a buzzard, for example. Good karma might enable an outcaste to be reborn as a Brahmin.
- **C.** To be reborn as a god or a Brahmin or, in some senses, simply as a human being was extremely rare and required a great deal of karmic merit.
- **D.** What made rebirth as a human so precious was that humans could positively affect their future existence. Animals, in contrast, weren't capable of generating much karma, which

meant that they couldn't greatly affect their rebirths. Humans, however, had almost limitless opportunities to act morally, that is, to produce karmically relevant deeds.

II. In the pre-Axial era, the Indo-Aryans weren't obsessively concerned about death. But that perspective changed significantly when the concept of *samsara*, or multiple rebirths, became adopted. One of the facets of rebirth is that *samsara* is not a desirable situation.

A. Most people who believed in reincarnation didn't want to be reborn because even the best possible life is fraught with suffering, pain, and grief and eventually ends in death.

B. It may take a million more lifetimes, but individuals would eventually realize the futility of samsaric existence. In the end, one must seek the ultimate aim of life: liberation from *samsara* altogether.

C. The Hindus call this liberation *moksha*, complete release—the end of reincarnation.

D. From the samsaric standpoint, endless lifetimes and the prospect of infinitely more caused Indians in the Axial Age to reconsider the value of the material world

III. As the idea of *samsara* spread, it spurred individuals to leave their families and jobs to seek a way to escape rebirth. This mass movement included men and women of all ages and castes but especially attracted those from the upper and middle castes.

A. It was during this period (800–400 B.C.E.) that Aryan culture became settled in towns. Farming and commerce flourished, and more people enjoyed material prosperity during a time of economic, social, and religious activity.

B. Traditional practices and beliefs were no longer taken for granted. The power of the Brahmin priests was called into question, and many people became dissatisfied with the shape of the new culture.

C. There was also a yearning for high adventure, for the quest of the perfect life that few dared to try. Those who joined the homeless and ascetic life saw in renunciation their only hope for freedom and fulfillment.

D. Sages believed that by perfecting the spiritual life, the samsaric realm might be conquered to achieve even greater bliss.

E. Many of these *samanas*, as they were called, lived alone in caves or forests; some lived with their families in ascetic communities; some wandered from village to village carrying only a change of clothes and a bowl used to beg for food.

F. So large and so familiar was this countercultural movement that the *samanas* were virtually regarded as a fifth caste, alongside priests, warriors, producers, and servants. Others sought out these ascetics for advice and lessons for living.

G. The relationship between ascetics and ordinary people became symbiotic. Non-ascetics gained good karma by giving to ascetics food, clothing, and shelter. Ascetics needed the support of ordinary folk to make their quest for *moksha* possible.

H. There was an intensely experimental quality to this period in Indian religious history. *Samanas* wandered from place to place seeking various gurus, trying different disciplines, and adopting diverse doctrines. Meditation, hatha yoga, and countless varieties of self-denial and self-mortification arose during this time.

I. Teachers competed for the allegiance of students and lay followers. Debates were held, conversations became heated, and rivalries were common. The intensity and energy of these competitions point to the profound importance and urgency of the quest.

IV. Though their lifestyles and beliefs varied widely, ascetics were united in their quest for relief from *samsara* and the belief that freedom lay in acquiring knowledge.

A. Knowledge had always played an important role in Vedic religion. But in the Axial Age, the quest for knowledge was urged on by the desire to know the deep reality that was the foundation for the whole of life.

B. The quest was for a knowledge that was comprehensive and fundamental. It was no longer enough to know the correct words to chant and rituals to perform. *Samanas* wanted to understand the deepest principles of reality.

C. The trend to view the world, not as collection of unrelated objects and beings, but as an integrated totality that could be understood by knowing its fundamental basis was so pervasive that this effort is seen as one of the salient characteristics of the Axial Age.

D. The sages searched for the key to the basic forces in the cosmos, hoping to reduce them to a singular principle, thus affording genuine freedom and fulfillment.

E. This knowledge was necessarily extraordinary and could only be gained by rigorous methods of asceticism and introspection, not transmitted through lectures or read from books.

F. Many of these ascetic seekers claimed to have found the way to final liberation, the answer to life's deepest questions, the knowledge of the secrets of the universe itself.

Essential Reading:

Sharma, *Classical Hindu Thought*, chapters 14–16.

Supplementary Reading:

Huyler, *Meeting God*, chapter 9.

Questions to Consider:

1. What was the fundamental force in motivating people to become ascetics during the Axial Age?
2. What are the chief differences in the quest for knowledge between early Indo-Aryans and the sages of the Axial Age?

Lecture Eight—Transcript
The Quest for Liberation

So far, we've observed the development of two key ideas about the nature and destiny of human beings that arose in India during the early Axial Age. The first was rebirth, the concept that our present earthly existence is only one in a series of lifetimes; the second was karma, the belief that our deeds have positive or negative consequences that return to the agent according to the nature of the act. Both conceptions were presented for the first time in the collection of writings called the Upanishads.

At first, rebirth and karma were not consistently understood by the many authors of this collection. There wasn't even universal agreement as to what these terms meant—much less agreement as to whether or not they existed. But there was a swarm of theories and speculations. Reading the Upanishads sometimes reminds me of those late night bull sessions that college students often have, where they try out new ideas with one another in part to see how others respond and in part to see how they themselves feel in saying such things. Such sessions are marked by a great deal of conjecture and experimentation, and it's not always clear that people are talking about the same things.

Over time, though, a basic pattern of belief began to emerge among the sages who were speculating on these matters. As we noted in our last talk, that pattern involved the ethicization of rebirth, the concept that moral deeds determine one's status at reincarnation. Good behavior yields a favorable rebirth; wicked behavior results in an unfavorable rebirth. "The Supreme Teaching," one of the earliest of the Upanishads, puts it quite simply, "What a man turns out to be depends on how he acts and conducts himself. If his actions are good, he will turn into something good. If his actions are bad, he will turn into something bad."

The doctrine of karma means that the status of your rebirth is in your hands. Karma makes the individual the master of his or her destiny. What happens to you is the consequences of your own choices and behavior. By the same token, your present condition was shaped by the deeds you performed previously. So like Zoroaster, the Upanishads elevate the importance of personal, moral responsibility.

To speak of a good or bad rebirth implies a hierarchy of being. One might be reborn at any level on this hierarchy, ranging from plant life to the various levels of animal life, to the human realm—which, of course, is stratified from low caste to high caste—and then to the various levels of divinity. A preponderance of bad karma might take you from being a human to being a buzzard: an abundance of good karma might enable the outcaste to be reborn as a Brahmin.

To have a high birth—that is, to be reborn as a god or a Brahmin or, in some senses, as simply a human being—is extremely rare and requires a great deal of karmic merit. For the vast portion of our infinite number of rebirths, most of us have been reborn as insects or other animal forms. That we have achieved a human rebirth in this life is a wondrous, almost miraculous occurrence, because it's such a difficult feat.

An ancient parable from this era makes the point in a very vivid way. The parable invites us to imagine that the entire world is covered with water, and that floating on the water's surface is a yoke with a single hole, like a collar to harness an ox. An eastern wind pushes the yoke west; a western wind pushes the yoke east. A southern wind drives it north; a northern wind drives it south. So the yoke is constantly moving. Now suppose a blind sea turtle lived in this vast ocean and came to the surface once every one hundred years. How often do you think that blind sea turtle, coming to the surface once every hundred years, would stick his neck into the yoke with a single hole? The parable suggests that a human rebirth occurs with the same frequency.

The Tibetans, who inherited one of the Indian views on rebirth, frequently refer to this existence as this precious human birth. What makes it so precious is not just its rarity, but also its significance in the grand scheme of things. Humans—more than other animals or even the gods—have the ideal opportunity for positively affecting their future existence. One of the reasons beings spend a great number of lifetimes at the animal level is that animals simply aren't capable of generating much karma—good or bad. And that means that those beings are not in a position to greatly affect their rebirth one way or another. But human beings, by the nature of their very makeup, have almost limitless opportunities to act morally, and that is, to produce karmically relevant deeds. To squander this precious human life would be tragic to say the least.

It is possible that the ideas of rebirth and karma may have risen independently of one another; but if so, it is clear they came to be inextricably linked in the Indian imagination during the Axial Age. When that connection was made, and then widely accepted throughout India, a whole new attitude towards life came to pervade their view of the world.

In the pre-Axial era, the Indo-Aryans took delight in the pleasures of this life and they beseeched their gods for the goods that could make their lives more comfortable and more enjoyable. They weren't obsessively concerned about death, but when they thought about it, death was more or less accepted as a fact of life and perhaps as the transition to an agreeable existence in heaven. But that Indo-Aryan perspective changes significantly when the concept of samsara is generally adopted.

One of the first facets of the theory of rebirth that has to be grasped—and this is especially true for those of us living in the west—is that samsara is not a desirable situation. Most people who believe in reincarnation do not want to be reborn. Of course, there are folks around who actually hope for rebirth. Usually, those who look forward to rebirth somehow imagine a continued existence like the current (and probably fairly privileged) life they now enjoy. They don't usually think of themselves as living as an aardvark, or a cockroach, or imagine themselves as lunch for a tiger in the jungle. But because the ancient Indians were closer to the natural world than most modern people are, they were probably very much aware of such possibilities.

Yet no matter how confident one is that his or her good behavior is sufficient to merit better and better rebirths, there comes a point when one realizes that even the best possible life is fraught with suffering, pain, and grief and must eventually end in death. Just reaching the top of the great chain of being, therefore, cannot be the ultimate goal. Even at the top of the hierarchy, rebirth continues without end. The good karma we have acquired will eventually exhaust itself and reincarnation is inevitable, along with the suffering that accompanies every life.

It may take a million more lifetimes, but Hindus believe that the individual will eventually become convinced of the futility of samsaric existence as a whole. In the end, one must seek for the ultimate aim of life: liberation from samsara all together. The Hindus call this *moksha*, complete release, the ending of reincarnation. Seeking a favorable rebirth can thus only be a preliminary goal. One hopes to maximize his or her good karma, steadily improving rebirth until one has attained a life in which realizing *moksha* is a possibility.

From the point of view I've been describing, existence does not seem so pleasant. To be sure, the worldly life has its pleasures: the warmth of family and children, the joys of eating good food and seeing beautiful sights, the love of friends and companions. But now from the samsaric standpoint, from the point of view of an endless number of previous lifetimes and the prospect of infinitely more, this world does not carry quite the same attraction for Indians in the Axial period as it did to the Indo-Aryans centuries before. Recall the words of Nachiketas to the King of Death, "All these pleasures pass away, O End of all! They weaken the power of life. … Man cannot be satisfied with wealth. Shall we enjoy wealth with you in sight? Shall we live while you are in power?"

The idea of samsara thus brings with it a new religious problematic: how to attain *moksha* and escape the endless round of rebirths all together. This was the fundamental problem of Indian religion of the Axial Age. Virtually every school of philosophy and every religious sect—and there have been many throughout the history of India—each in their own way tried to understand and solve this issue.

As the idea of samsara caught on in the Axial period, it spurred a widespread movement of individuals who decided that nothing in this world compared to the necessity of ending samsaric existence. So they left their homes and families and jobs to seek a way to escape rebirth. This mass movement included men and some women, of all ages and castes, but it tended to attract persons from the middle castes especially. For the most part, the principal activity took place in the years between 800 and 400 B.C.E. in the plains area of the Ganges River, in northeastern India, where the Indo-Aryan culture had expanded many years earlier.

I referred to this expansion into the Gangetic area previously as the second urbanization of India. It was during this period that Aryan culture became settled through the development of villages and towns. Farming and commerce flourished, and more people came to enjoy material prosperity. Over a dozen small republics and small kingdoms emerged. It was a time of economic, social, as well as religious ferment. Modern historians consider this period to be of such significance that it may have been, to quote one of them, the "most decisive phase for the development of Indian culture."

This was a world of change. Traditional practices and beliefs were no longer taken for granted. At least in this area of India, the Brahmin priests no longer enjoyed the power and prestige that they had in years earlier. Undoubtedly, many of those who joined this new movement were beginning to experience dissatisfaction with the shape this new culture was taking. One individual who left home during this period to join this ascetic movement described his motivation this way, many years after fact:

> It occurred to me that life in the home is cramped and dirty, while the life gone forth into homelessness is wide open; it is difficult to live a spiritual life completely perfect and pure in all its parts while cabined inside.

In these words we hear a discontentment with ordinary domestic existence, but we also hear a yearning for high adventure, for the quest of the perfect life that very few persons ever dare try. In other words, those who joined the homeless and ascetic life did not do so just to escape a world they found abhorrent, but because they saw in renunciation their only hope for a life of freedom and fulfillment. For this reason I would characterize the new Axial outlook in India as ultimately optimistic, despite its negative assessment of the phenomenal world. Although the world as we know it is indeed a vale of tears, the sages were saying, by perfecting the spiritual life, the samsaric realm might be conquered and an even greater bliss enjoyed. That was the conclusion of the individual who left home because it was cramped and dirty, the man who later became known as the Buddha.

Many of these *samanas*, as they were commonly known, lived alone in caves or in the forests; some lived with their families in ascetic communities; many wandered from village to village carrying only a change of clothes and a bowl for begging for food, (a pattern, by the way, still very much in evidence in India today). The householders—those who did not leave their homes and places in society—were still very much aware of these ascetics and sages. They were common sights in the villages and towns, and often the householders sought them out for advice and lessons for living. So large and so familiar was this countercultural movement that the *samanas* were virtually regarded as a fifth caste, alongside the priests, the warriors, the producers, and the servants.

The relationship between these ascetics and the ordinary householders became quite symbiotic, since the holy men and women needed the support of the ordinary folk to make their quest for liberation possible. Supporting the ascetics and renouncers by giving them food, and clothing, and shelter came to be seen as meritorious, as a way of gaining good karma. The ordinary householder might help the *samanas* now, in this life, knowing that in a future lifetime others would help him or her in his or her effort to attain *moksha*.

This emerging relationship between the *samanas* and the householders established an important difference in the respective religious orientations of these two groups. The *samanas* sought *moksha* in this very lifetime. But the householders—those who retained their roles in society, living a conventional life involving work and family—could not afford to devote their time and energies to the pursuit of *moksha*, and so they chose to postpone that endeavor until a later lifetime, when circumstances would favor it. In the meantime, the householder's goal was to improve the status of rebirth through the accumulation of positive karmas. So while liberation from samsara is the ultimate goal, not everyone seeks it in this life.

There was an intensely experimental quality to this period in Indian religious history. Individuals often wandered from place to place, seeking this guru or that holy man, trying now one form of discipline and now another, adopting this doctrine and then that. It was at this time that many of the practices that we've come to associate with Indian religion were developed and refined—disciplines such as meditation, and hatha yoga, and the countless varieties of self-denial and self-mortification, from fasting and celibacy to actually standing on one leg and lying on a bed of nails.

Teachers competed with one another for the allegiance of students and lay followers. Debates were held; conversations became heated; rivalries were common. Oftentimes, this competitiveness seemed to contain little of the spiritual or enlightened perspective in it. But the intensity and the competitive energy of these times also points to the profound importance and urgency of the quest. Probably not all *samanas* were pursuing their paths for noble ideals. Surely, some of them were simply following a fad or trying to escape responsibility at home. Who knows? But the ascetic life was a very difficult one and not many would pursue it without counting the costs.

The lifestyles and beliefs of this fifth caste varied widely, but they were united in their quest for relief from the acute sense of suffering implied by their understanding of samsara. And they were united in another way as well: in the belief that the way to freedom lay in acquiring knowledge. Their renunciation of the world is perhaps best seen in this light: as a necessary course of action for removing the impediments that might prevent them from getting the extraordinary knowledge that would win them *moksha*. The search for the knowledge to freedom was so important and *so* demanding that all worldly concerns had to be set aside.

Knowledge had always played a role in Vedic religion. It was central to the success of Aryan rituals that the priests know what they needed to do and how to speak the sacrificial formulas without error. Practitioners of Vedic rituals had to study for over a dozen years to gain the understanding necessary to function as priests. So it's not surprising that knowledge was initially emphasized in this growing movement.

But in the Axial Age, the quest for knowledge took a different turn, urged on by the new goal of liberation from samsara. It was not simply the knowledge of ritual action and the sacred words that was being sought. Such knowledge could only be useful in acquiring worldly goods or a brief respite in heaven. Now, the sages wanted to know the deep reality that was at the basis of ritual practice, and that meant the reality that was the foundation for the whole of life.

Their search for this kind of knowledge was different from the forms of knowing stressed in earlier manifestations of Indian religion. In the first place, the Axial Age quest was for a knowledge that was comprehensive and fundamental. It was no longer enough simply to know the correct words to chant and the ritual actions to perform: the *samanas* wanted to understand the whole of reality by understanding its deepest principles. The composer of the Mundaka Upanishad wonders: "What is that which, being known, illuminates everything else?"

And we see similar questions throughout the Axial centers. Zoroaster had essentially provided such knowledge to his followers with his vision of life as a cosmic clash between good and evil, which furnished a comprehensive framework for interpreting every aspect of existence and provided a practical way for orienting people's lives. Knowing that Mazda and the Evil One were struggling for control of the universe, it illuminated everything else. We'll witness similar efforts when we explore the emerging religions of South and East Asia. The trend to view the world not as a collection of unrelated objects and beings but as an integrated totality that can be understood by knowing its fundamental basis was so pervasive that we can designate this effort as one of the salient characteristics of the Axial Age.

And like other aspects of the Axial Age, this aspiration to understand the world's fundamental basis is still very much a part of the human thirst for knowledge. The desire to grasp reality's elemental nature that we see in the Upanishads and elsewhere is not unlike, for example, modern physics' hope to discover a unified field theory, which physicists sometimes call the Theory of Everything. For decades, physicists have worked to reconcile the four basic forces in the cosmos and to understand them by a single mathematical formula, in essence reducing them to a singular principle. The goal of a unified field theory has been the Holy Grail for many physicists who believe that finding it will unlock some of the deepest mysteries of the universe. In their own way, the sages of the Upanishads—and other Axial Age thinkers—were trying to develop their own Theory of Everything. They wanted to understand it all, not because they valued knowledge for knowledge's sake, but because knowing the fundamental basis of existence, they believed, could bring genuine freedom and fulfillment. This was a knowledge that conferred liberation.

A second quality of the knowledge sought by the North Indian *samanas* was that it was extraordinary, to be gained by rigorous methods of asceticism and introspection, and not merely transmitted by lectures—like what I'm doing here—or gained from reading books. The Sanskrit word for this form of knowledge is *jnana*, which is closely related to the Greek word *gnosis*. Many of you will recognize gnosis as the word for that esoteric understanding that was sought by some early Christians and others called, aptly enough, the Gnostics.

In the same way, the Indian *samanas* sought a super mundane kind of knowing, one that was in principle accessible to everyone but gained only by those willing to make the sacrifices required to get it. Because Indian philosophy had this pragmatic quality to it—almost always involving spiritual discipline and practice—it's difficult, if not impossible, to separate the realms of religion and philosophy in these traditions.

Despite the difficulty, despite the costs—or perhaps because of them—many of these ascetic seekers claimed to have found what they were looking for: the way to final liberation; the answer to life's deepest questions; the knowledge of the secrets of the universe itself.

We've now set forth the basic existential predicament of Indian religion, so we are now in a position to begin our study of some of the answers proposed by these ancient *samanas*. The religious excitement of the early Axial Age was marked by a wide variety of competing beliefs and practices, teachers and schools of thought. Although we have no record of many of these teachings, we know a great deal about the more prominent ones. Beginning with the next lecture, we will examine the solutions offered by three of the most important and enduring perspectives emerging from this North Indian renaissance. The first is the *Vedanta*, the views offered by the Upanishads themselves, which provide a basic theological foundation for Hinduism. Then we take up Buddhism and Jainism, two traditions that reinterpret the problem of samsara and then offer an alternative answer to the classical Hinduism approaches.

Well, I've just promised to reveal the ways to liberation and the secrets of the cosmos. I'm sure these will be lectures you won't want to miss!

Lecture Nine
The Vedantic Solution

Scope:

For many ascetics, the quest for liberation focused on discovering the knowledge of ultimate reality and the self. The results of their search are disclosed in the ancient collection of texts known as the Upanishads. Recorded in these texts are the speculations of generations of Axial Age sages. The general viewpoint of the Upanishads is that the soul is invisible and immortal, never created and never destroyed, and separate from both the body and the mind. Eventually, the Upanishads reaches the conclusion that the soul is identical with Brahman, the deepest reality, far beyond the reach of concepts, words, or any other product of the human mind. *Atman* and Brahman are simply different words for the same reality. *Maya*, or illusion, leads us to act as if individuality were real, but in fact, there is only one reality, and that is *atman*-Brahman. To realize the Absolute thus entails penetrating *maya*'s veil and acknowledging the identity of the self and ultimate reality.

Outline

I. The Upanishads were the first texts to offer a solution to the problem of *samsara* through Vedanta, a principal branch of Hindu philosophy. In seeking to unlock the deepest mysteries of existence, end the samsaric cycle, and bring about utter bliss, sages sought two particular bits of knowledge. One was the nature of the self and the discovery of what lies deep within the individual as his or her essence. We focus first on this essence.

- **A.** The vast majority of religions and philosophies of the last 3,000 years have asserted that the human essence is something more than our material bodies. Religion gives various names to this essence, such as *self*, *spirit*, *mind*, *heart*, and *soul*.
- **B.** The Sanskrit word for "soul" is *atman*, an ancient Vedic term that was reinterpreted in the Axial Age.
- **C.** In the early Vedas, the *atman* was closely associated with breath. By the time the Upanishads had begun to be

composed, however, the breath was seen as too physical, too closely associated with the body.

D. The sages of the Upanishads sought to define the soul as something that transcended the body and survived death, in other words, an immortal substance.

E. Some authors suggested that the mind or consciousness was the soul. But almost all of the Upanishadic sages were reluctant to agree because of the mind's capriciousness and unsettled nature.

F. Some sages believed that what is beyond the senses and the mind itself could not be sensed or thought about. From this insight, the Upanishads derived the unique quality of the soul—that it must be beyond comprehension.

G. Because the soul transmigrated from body to body through rebirth, the *atman* must also be immortal. It is not created; it simply always has been.

H. Upanishadic thinkers didn't all agree on the specific details of the human self, but they all subscribed to a general understanding that distinguished a higher self from a lower self.

1. The lower—*phenomenal*—self comprised the body, the senses, and the mind. These aspects are all transitory and mortal.
2. The higher self—*atman*—was distinguishable from these other elements by virtue of its eternal and spiritual nature. Confusing the higher with the lower self is what brings anguish to the human condition.

II. Just as Indian thinkers sought to understand the nature of the self, they also wanted to comprehend the ultimate reality, the fundamental power or principle supporting all there is, which would also free them from *samsara*.

A. Like the quest for the soul, the sages' pursuit of ultimate reality was founded on an idea from the old Vedas, rooted in the Brahmins' mysterious power hidden within ritual—Brahman.

B. By the Axial Age, Brahman had come to mean more than the power of ritual; it now referred to ultimate reality itself, which was a logical development in Indo-Aryan religion.

1. The ritual and its sacred words had always been understood to correspond to greater cosmological and moral realities beyond the simple ceremony itself.
2. The story of the sacrifice of Purusha suggested that society, various elements of the world, ritual practices, and the Sanskrit language itself were all intrinsically and mystically connected to one another. Seeking the deeper meaning to the nature of existence by understanding Brahman was a natural outcome of this line of thinking.

C. Sages didn't agree about the exact nature of Brahman, but they did agree that Brahman is one undifferentiated unity with no parts or divisions.

D. Brahman is said to permeate all things but cannot be perceived. It embraces good and evil yet transcends both. Paradoxically, it encompasses the whole of reality yet surpasses it.

1. However, Brahman was not the same as god, a supreme being. More aptly, it was described as the Absolute or being itself. These words obviously do not tell us much or give us concrete images with which to conceive of Brahman, but that is precisely the point.
2. Brahman thus transcends all human categories and images; Hindu theologians defined Brahman as *nirguna*, "without qualities."

E. Gradually, the Upanishadic sages came to realize that Brahman was ultimately unknowable, at least in the conventional sense. Brahman eluded conception and perception, and thus, these faculties were ineffective in discovering the absolute reality.

III. As the sages of the Upanishads continued their quest of the human essence and ultimate reality—the mystical—an epiphany emerged in the later Upanishads. The concepts of *atman* and Brahman converged such that the soul was seen as identical to ultimate reality itself, one and the same, and to believe otherwise was the source of our misery.

A. In addition to their assertion that the soul carried a divine spark, the sages believed that *atman* and Brahman were two names for the same reality. The true self *is* ultimate reality; therefore, Brahman-*atman* is the only reality there is.

B. Despite the Upanishads' exalted view of humanity, the soul still finds itself in an endless cycle of death and rebirth, seeking ever-new manifestations until it finds its rest in God.

C. The Upanishads address the seemingly contradictory claim that Brahman and *atman* are one and the same yet the soul still suffers from *samsara*, by stating that *samsara* is a consequence of our ignorance and misunderstanding of reality.

D. *Maya* is the veil over reality that accounts for our ignorance, causing us to perceive and conceive of the world as composed of many different things rather than the one reality it is.

E. *Maya* also deceives us into thinking of ourselves as separate entities, individuals separate from one another and from ultimate reality.

F. *Maya* causes us to forget who we truly are and prompts us to identify with our lower selves, thus trapping us in *samsara* until we fully recognize the truth about Brahman and *atman*.

G. People tend to think and act in self-centered ways, focusing on desires and deeds that perpetuate the illusion of our separateness from Brahman. This sense of separateness engenders fear and hatred, greed for material goods and power, and ultimately, fear of death.

Essential Reading:

Mascaró, *The Upanishads*.

Supplementary Reading:

Hopkins, *The Hindu Religious Tradition*, chapter 3.

Brereton, "The Upanishads," in *Approaches to the Asian Classics*, de Bary and Bloom, eds.

Questions to Consider:

1. What qualities distinguish humans from other animals?
2. How might early Axial Age sages have concluded that the nature of reality and the nature of the soul (Brahman and *atman*) were one and the same? What are the theological benefits and liabilities of this identification?

3. How did Brahman come to be considered ultimate reality itself?

Lecture Nine—Transcript
The Vedantic Solution

In the early centuries of the Axial period, vast numbers of individuals in northeastern India began to renounce their ties to society and head for the forests and mountains to seek liberation from samsara. It was out this movement that the religions of Hinduism, Buddhism, and Jainism all began to develop and assume their distinctive characteristics. Although these three traditions understood the details of rebirth differently, they all believed that the seemingly endless rounds of existence was the central problem of life. They all agreed, furthermore, that the end to the cycle of rebirths was indeed within human grasp, as long as the individuals were fully dedicated to the task. None of them thought the path would be easy. Yet, despite these common convictions, they each offered different solutions to the problem of *samsara*.

Over the next several lectures, we'll examine these various approaches and movements that they set in motion, beginning now with Vedanta, and the perspective offered by the Upanishads themselves. The Upanishads were not only the first texts to set forth the new problematic for the Axial Age; they were also the first texts to offer a solution to that problem.

In due course, Hinduism added other spiritual pathways to its immense repertoire of practices and doctrines, so it would not be accurate to say that Vedanta is the Hindu solution. Like everything else in Hinduism, it's one among many. In fact, it doesn't even represent the most popular form of spirituality in present-day Hinduism. Nonetheless, Vedanta is probably the form of Hinduism that westerners are most familiar with, since the first interpreters of Hinduism to the west were either Hindu practitioners of Vedanta or westerners who were enamored with its philosophy. But despite its minority status among modern Hindus, the Vedantic way was crucial for the genesis and subsequent evolution of Hinduism. Because it develops many of the basic concepts accepted by almost all varieties of Hinduism, this theological perspective informs the religious lives of those Hindus who do not directly practice it.

The Upanishads were composed by sages seeking to unlock the deepest mysteries of existence. Essentially, they wanted to know two things: the nature of ultimate reality and the nature of the self.

Apprehending these, they believed, would confer the liberating knowledge that would halt the samsaric cycle and bring about a state of utter bliss. We could say that the Upanishads take two seemingly opposite trajectories: one in the direction of comprehending the universe in its greatest possible sense—that is, in knowing the fundamental power or principle underlying the totality of the world; the other in the direction of discovering what lies deep within the individual as his or her essence. We will discuss both of these lines of inquiry, beginning with the latter issue first, the nature of selfhood.

I saw a bumper sticker once that admonished its readers to "Never forget that you are unique—just like everyone else!" Well, of course, we're all unique; but then, there's nothing unique about being unique. We human beings do like to think we're special, whether as individuals or as a species. We want to believe that there is something about *us* that sets us apart from everything else. In the book of Genesis, for instance, the god Yahweh creates all the animals simply by calling them into existence, but when it comes to the human, he personally fashions a body made of dust and then breathes into it the breath of life. Yahweh's animating breath and particular attention differentiates humans from the other animals and makes us special.

This example from Genesis is not unique, either. Almost all creation narratives reserve special treatment for humans. I'm not absolutely sure about this, but other animals don't seem to be as obsessed with themselves as humans are. In fact, I know of no other creature that dwells so much on what they are and what they should be. For millennia, we human beings have wondered about ourselves and about what gives us life and determines our qualities. We've spent enormous amounts of intellectual energy trying to understand the essence of being human, what it is that makes us different from other beings and perhaps different from one other. But, hey, I'm not complaining: this human drive is what makes my job possible. Perhaps that drive in itself is part of our essential natures: we are the animals who must interpret ourselves.

The vast majority of religions and philosophies of the last 3,000 years have said that the human essence is something more than our material bodies. They've given various names to this essence, such as self, spirit, mind, heart; but the most common word may be soul.

There has rarely been much precision about what they believe this essence actually is, but these terms—and others like them—are what religions and philosophies have used to indicate that aspect of being—whatever it might be—that animates and gives life to our bodies and signifies what we truly are.

The sages who composed the Upanishads also used the word soul, to designate the human essence. The actual Sanskrit word was *atman*. Like the idea of karma, *atman* was an ancient Vedic term that was reinterpreted and redefined in the Axial Age. In the earlier Vedas, the *atman* was closely associated with breath. The German verb meaning to breathe is *atmen*, spelled almost exactly the same as the Sanskrit. The Vedic notion that the breath might be the human essence was based on the rather commonsensical view that since the breath leaves the body at death, breath must be the animating force of life. But by the time the Upanishads had begun to be composed, the identification of *atman* with breath was unsatisfying to most thinkers. The breath was seen as too physical, too closely associated with the body. In one of the Upanishads, the great god Indra is depicted as worried about this association. In response to a *samana* who claims that body and soul are identical, Indra reasons:

> If our self, our [soul], is the body, and is dressed in clothes of beauty when the body is, then when the body is blind, the [soul] is blind, and when the body is lame, the [soul] is lame; and when the body dies, the [soul] dies. I cannot find any joy in this doctrine.

What the sages of the Upanishads sought as the soul was something that transcends the body and survives death—in other words, an immortal substance. Part of the context of this passage, of course, was the increasing anxiety about the fate of the individual at death, one of the major themes of the Axial transformation.

If not the body or the breath, what does constitute the human essence? What is the soul? Some authors suggested the mind or consciousness. The mind, for many of us, seems to be the center of our personality, but almost all of the Upanishadic sages were reluctant to identify the human essence with mind or consciousness. "How can anything as capricious and as unsettled as the mind be our immortal self?" they asked. One of the earlier Upanishads says: "It is not the mind that we should want to know; we should want to know the thinker." What was of greatest interest was not the content or the activity of the mind, but what existed beneath or beyond it.

Some of the sages concluded that what is beyond the senses and the mind itself could not be sensed or thought about. From this insight, the Upanishads derive the unique qualities of the soul: the *atman* itself must be imperceptible, beyond the categories of thinking, and beyond comprehension. Although the soul dwells within the body, it is different from the body and all its parts. Because it transmigrates from body to body through rebirth, the *atman* must also be immortal. The Katha Upanishad puts it this way:

> *Atman*, the spirit of vision, is never born and never dies. Before him there was nothing, and he is one for evermore. Never born, eternal, beyond times gone or times to come, he does not die when the body dies. If the slayer thinks that he kills; if the slain thinks that he dies, neither knows the ways of truth. The Eternal in humanity cannot kill; the Eternal in humanity cannot die.

The *atman* does not come into being at a specifiable moment. It's not created; it simply always has been.

We might contrast this view with the position of many western religions who've recently dealt with the question of the soul's creation while struggling with the issue of abortion. Roman Catholicism contends that the soul is created at conception; some Protestant groups have said that it starts 14 days after conception; a Jewish tradition says that it's 40 days after conception for boys and 90 days after for girls; and Islam maintains that an angel breathes the life-force into the fetus 120 days into pregnancy. Although they disagree on the exact moment of ensoulment, the western traditions are fundamentally together in saying that the soul comes into being at a particular moment in time.

Similarly, the Upanishadic thinkers are not of one accord in the specific details of their views of the human self, but they all subscribe to a general understanding that distinguishes a higher self from a lower self. The lower or phenomenal self comprises the body, and the senses, and the mind. These aspects are all transitory and mortal. The higher self, or *atman*, is distinguishable from these other elements by virtue of its eternal and spiritual nature. Confusing the higher with the lower self, in fact, is much of what brings anguish to the human condition.

Just as Indian thinkers sought to understand the nature of the self, they also wanted to comprehend ultimate reality, the fundamental power or principle supporting all there is. Like the quest for the soul, the sages' pursuit of ultimate reality was founded on an idea from the old Vedas, which was reinterpreted during the Axial period. This particular notion was rooted in the Brahmins' speculation about what made the sacrifice effective. You'll recall that the Vedas used a specific technical term to refer to the mysterious power that lies hidden within the ritual: they called it *Brahman*, and the Brahmin caste believed their principal function was to ensure its proper application.

In the Axial period, the quest for liberating knowledge came to focus on discovering the true nature of this Brahman. The focus on Brahman actually follows a fairly logical development in Indo-Aryan religion. The ritual and its sacred words had always been understood to correspond to greater cosmological and moral realities beyond the simple ceremony itself. The story of the sacrifice of the Purusha that we discussed in an earlier talk suggested that society, the various elements of the world, the ritual practices, and the Sanskrit language itself were all mystically connected to one another. Seeking the deeper meaning to the nature of existence by understanding Brahman was only the natural outcome of this line of thinking. By the Axial Age, Brahman had come to mean more than the power of ritual; it now referred to ultimate reality itself.

The authors of the Upanishads, however, were not in complete agreement about the exact nature of Brahman. But there was at least one thing on which there seemed to be fundamental agreement. Throughout the Upanishads, we are told that Brahman is one, a singular, undifferentiated unity. There are no parts or divisions to Brahman. In various other passages, Brahman is credited with creating and sustaining the world and all life. It's sometimes called the thread that strings together all creatures. Brahman is said to permeate all things but it cannot be perceived. It embraces good and evil and yet transcends both. It's beyond morality altogether. In short, Brahman encompasses the whole of reality and yet surpasses it. There is nothing beyond the scope of Brahman.

At this level, it would be misleading, I think, to identify Brahman with god, if by god we mean a supreme being. Brahman is not a being, and certainly not a personal being; hence it's referred to with impersonal pronouns such as it, rather than as he or she. Brahman would be more aptly described as the absolute or being-itself. These words obviously do not tell us much or give us concrete images with which to conceive Brahman, but that's precisely the point.

This excerpt from the Isha Upanishad captures the sense of the magnificence and elusiveness of Brahman:

> [Brahman], without moving, is swifter than the mind; the senses cannot reach it: It is ever beyond them. Standing still, it overtakes those who run. To the ocean of its being, the spirit of life leads the streams of action. It moves, and it moves not. It is far, and it is near. It is within all, and it is outside all. [Brahman] filled all with its radiance. It is incorporeal and invulnerable, pure and untouched by evil. It is…immanent and transcendent. It placed all things in the path of Eternity.

By means of paradox and negation, this passage asserts that Brahman transcends all human categories and images. By claiming that it moves and moves not, for instance, the author demonstrates how Brahman exhausts and depletes our categories for understanding it. How can it both move and not move? What kind of sense does that make? Well, it makes no sense according to our conventional forms of logic. The very point of such a phrase is to confound our thinking. Hindu theologians came to say that Brahman was *nirguna*, without qualities. To try to describe it in anything other than a paradoxical or negative way makes it into something that can be comprehended, which by definition, it cannot be.

Gradually, the Upanishadic sages came to realize that Brahman was ultimately unknowable, at least not knowable in the conventional sense of that word. Brahman, they believed, eluded conception and perception and so these faculties were ineffective in discovering the absolute reality. What they sought was the deepest kind of knowing, a grasp of reality that we can best call mystical or ineffable. An excerpt from the Kena Upanishad, one of the shortest of the principal Upanishads, describes the mystical features of this knowledge:

> What cannot be spoken with words, but that whereby words are spoken: Know that alone to be Brahman, the spirit, and not what people here adore.
>
> What cannot be thought with the mind, but that whereby the mind can think: Know that alone to be Brahman, the spirit, and not what people here adore.
>
> What cannot be seen with the eye, but that whereby the eye can see: Know that alone to be Brahman, the spirit, and not what people here adore.
>
> What cannot be heard with the ear, but that whereby the ear can hear: Know that alone to be Brahman, the spirit, and not what people here adore.
>
> What cannot be indrawn with the breath, but that whereby breath is indrawn: Know that alone to be Brahman, the spirit, and not what people here adore. …
>
> Sight does not reach there; neither does thinking or speech.
>
> We don't know, we can't perceive how one would point it out.
>
> It is far different from what's known.
>
> And it is farther than the unknown.

As the sages of the Upanishads continued their quests of the human essence and the ultimate reality, a new insight begins to break into awareness, an epiphany that came to full expression in the later Upanishads. As they increasingly appreciated the incomprehensible and unutterable nature of both Brahman and *atman*, these two ideas converged. The sages concluded that which is called soul is identical with ultimate reality itself. They are one and the same. The Upanishads express this insight in a variety of ways. One text asserts: "Who[ever] denies God, denies himself. Who[ever] affirms God, affirms himself."

The Chandogya Upanishad says this:

> This is the Spirit that is in my heart, smaller than a grain of rice, or a grain of barley, or a grain of mustard-seed, or a grain of canary-seed. This is the Spirit that is in my heart,

> greater than the earth, greater than the sky, greater than heaven itself, greater than all these worlds.

Another celebrated passage tells how a father named Uddalaka teaches this revelation to his son Svetaketu, a young man who has just completed his formal schooling but who apparently has missed out on the most important lesson of all. Uddalaka creates an object lesson by asking Svetaketu to take a fruit from the great banyan tree, to break it open, and dissect one of the seeds. Svetaketu does as he's told. When he finds his father and tells him that he sees nothing within, Uddalaka makes his point:

> My son, from the very essence in the seed which you cannot see comes in truth this vast banyan tree. Believe me, my son, an invisible and subtle essence is the Spirit of the whole universe. That is Reality. That is *Atman*. THOU ART THAT.

These passages are not merely claiming that the soul is a part of god or carries a divine spark or is created in the image of god. Rather, the identity of *atman* and Brahman means they are consubstantial, two names for the same reality. The true self *is* ultimate reality. Brahman-*atman* is the only reality there is.

It's hard to imagine a more exalted view of humanity. This assessment of the self seems almost diametrically opposite to that of mainstream of Western monotheism, in which god is viewed as wholly other than humanity, to use a phrase that was popular among early 20th-century Protestant theologians. Or, to cite the Christian theologian Søren Kierkegaard, there is an "infinite qualitative difference" between god and humanity.

Despite the Upanishads' lofty view, the soul nonetheless finds itself in an endless cycle of birth, death, and rebirth. Like many religious traditions west and east, the classical Hindu view understands that the embodied soul is not at rest; it's not in its true home. It continues in this restless state, seeking ever-new manifestations until it finds, as Augustine would say, its rest in God. So how do we reconcile these two seemingly contradictory claims? I mean on the one hand, our true selves are identical with the ultimate reality, absolutely the same; and yet on the other hand, we suffer the rounds of incessant rebirth. How can this be?

According to the Upanishads, samsara is a consequence of our ignorance, our misperception and misunderstanding of reality. The Upanishads speak of *maya*, a veil over reality that accounts for our ignorance. *Maya* causes us to perceive plurality when in reality there is unity. We perceive and conceive the world as composed of many things rather than the one reality that it is. *Maya* deceives us into thinking of ourselves as separate entities, as individuals, separate from one another, separate from ultimate reality. It causes us to forget who we truly are and prompts us to identify with our lower selves. But our lower selves, because they are transitory and inconstant, are ultimately not real.

Until we fully recognize the truth about Brahman and *atman*, we continue to suffer on the wheel of samsara, because we continue to generate karma that binds us to this phenomenal world. Believing ourselves to be individuals, we tend to act and think in self-centered ways, creating the desires and deeds that perpetuate the illusion of our separateness from Brahman. And it's this sense of separateness that engenders fear and hatred of others, the greed for material goods and power, and ultimately the fear of death.

The Maitri Upanishad says, "Whenever the soul has thoughts of 'I' and 'mine', it binds itself with its lower self, as a bird with the net of a snare." Paradoxically, the very desire to be special that we spoke of earlier is the source of our misery.

I'm well aware of an underlying irony to this entire lecture. I have spent the last half hour discussing a reality that by definition cannot be discussed. Whether we call it Brahman or *atman*, the referent of our terms is defined as something beyond mind, beyond concept, beyond language. And yet without concept, without language, this talk on ultimate reality in Hinduism would have been 30 minutes of complete silence.

The good thing about this irony from a pedagogical perspective is that gives me a great excuse if my lecture has been unclear or confusing. You still don't understand Brahman and *atman*? Well, don't blame me; those subjects can't be comprehended through words. The most lucid possible talk on Brahman and *atman* will never suffice to engender the kind of knowledge required for liberation, and until one attains such liberating knowledge, one has not realized ultimate reality. But if not through language, how is it that one comes to such an understanding? How does one penetrate the *maya* that deceives our minds and causes our unhappiness? That's what we'll explore in our next talk.

Lecture Ten
The One and the Many

Scope:

The realization of the identity of *atman* and Brahman required more than mere conceptual knowledge. To attain the knowledge that liberated one from *samsara*, it was essential to gain a deep, existential understanding wrought by various spiritual practices, including meditation and asceticism. These techniques were intended to turn the adept within, enabling him or her to dissociate from the "lower" self and identify with *atman*. This reorientation of identity allowed individuals to relinquish the desires that kept them bound to *samsara*.

But the Vedantic solution was not for everyone. Many found it too demanding or too rarefied. Ordinary people preferred a spirituality in which ultimate reality could be conceptualized and to which they could relate. Through the theology of Saguna Brahman, it was possible for the ultimate reality to be partially depicted through images without lapsing into idolatry. The Bhagavad-Gita, written late in the Axial Age, advanced this view of personal theism and asserted its consistency with the path of the Vedanta.

Outline

I. Two fundamentally different theologies and practices emerged during the Indian Axial period. One was the belief that ultimate reality is incomprehensible to ordinary consciousness. To attain complete awareness of Brahman and *atman*, different methods evolved among different practitioners.

- **A.** The Vedantic way insisted that truth could be found only within one's deepest self; to discover this was to discover the highest reality.
- **B.** One method of discovering the divine within is through the Hindu practice of meditation.
    - **1.** By the Axial Age, meditation had eclipsed ritual as the chief discipline for *samanas* seeking *moksha* (a state of equanimity toward the world). Restraining the body and

mind to achieve a state of inner stillness was most important.

2. When the mind was focused in meditation, one could avoid distracting thoughts and sensations.
3. Serious and regular meditation could bring about visions, ecstasy, intensified awareness, and transcendence of thoughts, which brought one to the higher self, or *atman*.

C. Meditation complemented the *samanas*' efforts to dissociate from the lower self. Some of the techniques were intended to close off avenues that led seekers astray, keeping them trapped in the net of *maya*.

D. Some ascetics took vows of silence, because the knowledge of Brahman was beyond language.

E. Some tried to overcome their attachments to the material world through poverty, fasting, and celibacy.

F. Others took more extreme measures, such as "mortifying" the body, which might include standing immobile for long periods of time, piercing the flesh, lying on a bed of nails, or practicing self-flagellation.

G. These varied practices were meant to train ascetics to give up all attachments that encourage a sense of individuality or separateness from the rest of reality.

H. To realize the higher self and its identity with Brahman, one had to relinquish all selfish desires. Desire created karma, and karma bound one to *samsara*.

II. For the Upanishadic sages, the true self had nothing to desire or fear. And because one lacked for nothing and feared nothing, taking this path brought about a deep sense of serenity and indescribable joy, beyond all earthly pleasures.

A. Breaking the cycle of *samsara* meant no rebirth, no clinging to life, no dread of dying, just a state of equanimity toward the world, called *moksha*.

B. Those who worked toward *moksha* were *jivanmuktas*—living, liberated souls.

C. Some texts refer to the experience of *moksha* as "merging with" or "returning to" Brahman, but those images mislead because the soul does not need to unite with Brahman if it already is Brahman.

D. Another paradox is that the *jivanmukta* must strive to reach liberation, but effort is not what accomplishes unity with Brahman. *Moksha* is less an achievement than it is a simple understanding of truth.

III. The Upanishads blended tantalizing and provocative ideas with just enough uncertainty to inspire successive generations to continue reinterpreting their essential features. Here, we uncover more philosophical problems of Vedanta.

A. One question to be explored is that if Brahman-*atman* is the only reality there is, why does the illusion of *maya* exist and how is it created?

B. Another logical problem arises: If there are no individuals, then there are no souls in the plural. But if there are no souls—only Brahman-*atman*—is transmigration real or is *samsara* itself an illusion?

C. Despite these questions, the Upanishads' significance to the overall Hindu tradition was that they established key elements that provided Hinduism with its many characteristic features:

1. The belief in the unity and the incomprehensibility of ultimate reality.
2. The notions of *samsara*, karma, *atman*, and *moksha*.
3. The sense that the world and ourselves are not really the way they appear.

IV. Despite its profound importance in the development of the Hindu tradition, the Vedantic perspective didn't satisfy everyone's religious sensibilities. As Hinduism evolved through the Axial period, new perspectives and practices were added to accommodate individual beliefs and tastes.

A. Hinduism became a family of religions without a creed or core of beliefs. It embraces differences rather than excluding them.

B. Hinduism recognized that people were at different stages in their spiritual lives, and the practices and beliefs of one person might not be suitable for another.

C. Many Indians found the Upanishads' path of knowledge too demanding and unappealing to live.

D. Most Hindus preferred a more traditional piety focused on worshiping personal gods and goddesses, as opposed to the highly abstract Brahman.

E. The worship of personal deities continued unabated in the Axial Age and became even more popular near its end with the composition of the Bhagavad-Gita, perhaps the most frequently read Hindu scripture.

V. In addition to the belief that ultimate reality is incomprehensible to ordinary consciousness, a second theistic view arose during the Indian Axial period. Here, we see the divine represented by symbols and images, allowing devotees to draw closer to the divine.

A. To incorporate the vast numbers of venerated gods and goddesses, Hinduism refined the theology of Brahman, providing a way for both the devotees of gods and the seekers of Brahman to understand that they were venerating the same ultimate reality.

B. Though the Upanishads clearly emphasized the incomprehensibility of Brahman (*nirguna*, or "without qualities"), later thinkers offered the idea of a partially knowable Brahman, called *Saguna Brahman*—or "one with qualities."

C. The many gods and goddesses of popular piety were now many manifestations of the one inconceivable reality, each a conduit to the ultimate reality.

VI. The Saguna Brahman acknowledges the individual need for a concrete focus, an image toward which each can orient his or her devotion, direct prayers, and grasp the nature of the ultimate reality. Throughout their history, Hindus have fashioned physical representations of their gods and goddesses to serve as centers of faith.

A. Hindu images can be anthropomorphic, appearing humanlike. To imagine ultimate reality as similar to us allows devotees to feel close to the highest reality.

B. Hindu images can also be non-anthropomorphic, taking the form of stones, trees, rivers, and celestial bodies.

C. The danger in personalizing the divine, however, is making it seem too human until it becomes unworthy of devotion. To avoid this danger, Hindu images incorporate non-human elements, such as half-human/half-animal features. These remind devotees that gods and goddesses are not like us.

D. When an icon is first handcrafted, elaborate rituals are sometimes performed to invite the god or goddess that the image represents to inhabit the icon. The consecrated image is treated as if it were alive; it is bathed, clothed, decorated, and offered food.

E. At specific times during the day, worshipers are offered a special viewing—*darśan*—of the divine image. Seeing the god or goddess and being seen by it is vastly important to Hindus.

F. Ordinarily, the incarnation of the god or goddess is only temporary, and the physical image is destroyed to remind devotees that the image itself is not the divine.

G. Even though the Hindu pantheon is immense—330 million gods and goddesses—individual Hindus do not worship them all. Each devotee has an *ista-devatā*, a personal deity of choice.

H. Some consider the religious use of images idol worship, but even religions that refer to the divine as "father" or "king" are, in essence, giving form to that which is ultimately formless. Unless one is absolutely silent about ultimate reality, it is not possible to avoid human-made images and concepts, whether physical or linguistic.

I. The idea of Nirguna Brahman, therefore, reminds devotees that the ultimate reality always transcends any image.

VII. The best resource for understanding the worship of Hindu gods is probably the Bhagavad-Gita, the popular scripture written at the end of the Axial Age.

A. Primarily a dialogue between the warrior Arjuna and the god Krishna, the Gita is a taste of Hinduism's many practices and beliefs, including Vedic rituals, karma and morality, meditation and yoga, and devotion to the gods. One of its central points is that all these disciplines are spiritually beneficial.

B. The Gita also suggests that devotion to god is the best practice of all. In it, Krishna encourages Arjuna to focus his mind, will, and heart on god and to let go of all else in order to find liberation from *samsara*.

C. All that matters is to do all things with faith in and dedication to god. The Gita says that faith can be so potent that it doesn't matter if one is devoted to the god Krishna by name. What matters is not the object of faith but its quality and sincerity.

Essential Reading:

Sharma, *Classical Hindu Thought*, chapters 1 and 3.

Supplementary Reading:

Huyler, *Meeting God*, chapters 1–2.

Questions to Consider:

1. The Western theistic traditions have generally resisted and often condemned physical images of the divine. The Second Commandment of the Hebrew Bible forbids the making of "graven images" (Exodus 20:4). Nonetheless, these same traditions are full of linguistic images and metaphors for god. Are there good reasons to prefer linguistic images over physical ones for understanding divine reality?
2. In what ways do monotheistic traditions tend toward polytheism? How might monotheism and polytheism be problematic categories?
3. What is the main difference between Saguna Brahman and Nirguna Brahman, and how does that affect one's pursuit of the divine?

Lecture Ten—Transcript
The One and the Many

According to the Upanishads, it's not enough for the mind to grasp the concepts of *atman* and Brahman. Merely knowing the identity of self and ultimate reality in a theoretical or conceptual way does little good unless it's apprehended by the core of one's being. Only then does it become the liberating knowledge that leads to *moksha*. Without this deep, existential understanding, one continues to live a life of self-centeredness and desire, generating the karma that binds us to *samsara*. Today, we'll explore what the sages of the Axial Age thought it took to gain this extraordinary kind of understanding and what the alternatives were for those who found this approach too difficult or simply unappealing.

Attaining the complete awareness of Brahman and *atman* involves, first of all, a reorientation to the discovery of truth. Whereas many religions encourage their followers to look for truth in a book or creed or rituals, the Vedantic perspective insists that the truth is not out there, but within, within one's deepest self. To discover one's self is to discover the highest reality. "He who has found and knows his Soul," says the Chandogya Upanishad, "has found all the worlds."

The discovery of the divine within is one of the aims of the introspective disciplines of Hinduism, particularly, meditation. Meditation was probably practiced in India long before the Axial Age. Some of the artifacts discovered in the ruins of the Indus culture depict individuals in what appears to be a traditional meditative pose. The Vedas, as well, suggest that the Indo-Aryans may have used a form of meditation. By the Axial Age, meditation had come to eclipse ritual as the chief discipline for samanas seeking *moksha*.

The various Upanishads recommend different methods for engaging in meditation, but there were some characteristics common to all of them. Of prime importance was restraining the body and the mind to achieve a state of inner stillness. Ordinarily, this objective involved sitting in an upright posture in a quiet place, free from distractions. Then the mind was focused on a particular object, such as the breath, or an external or internal image, or a mantra, a special word intoned silently to oneself. This focus helped the mind concentrate and avoid thoughts and sensations that distracted from the aim of the practice. Over time, serious and regular meditation was said to bring about an array of experiences, including visions, ecstasy, the intensification of awareness, and the transcendence of thoughts and imaginings. One of the Upanishads also promised "health…lightness of body, a pleasant scent, a sweet voice; and an absence of greedy desires." By the steady engagement of meditative techniques, one gained access to the higher self, to the *atman*.

The practice of meditation was complemented by the samanas' efforts to dissociate from the lower self, that is habitually mistaken for the genuine self. Some of the techniques were intended to close off avenues that led seekers astray, keeping them trapped in the net of *maya*, of illusion. Some ascetics took vows of silence to eliminate words, since the knowledge of Brahman was beyond language. Some tried to overcome their attachment to the material world by taking vows of poverty, and fasting, and celibacy. Others took more extreme measures involving mortifying the body, literally putting the flesh to death. Mortification techniques comprised a wide range of observances, including standing immobile for long periods of time, often years; piercing the flesh with sharp objects; lying on beds of nails; and self-flagellation. The point of all these practices—from the mild to the harsh—was to train the ascetic to give up all attachments that encourage a sense of individuality or separateness from the rest of reality. To realize the higher self and its identity with Brahman, one had to relinquish all selfish desires. The "Supreme Teaching" says, "When all desires that cling to the heart disappear, then a mortal becomes immortal, and even in this life attains Liberation." Desire creates karma, and karma binds one to *samsara*.

For the Upanishadic sages, to see the true self meant to see that there was nothing to desire and nothing to fear. If the *atman* were immortal and consubstantial with ultimate reality itself, what reason would there be to want or fear anything? And because one lacked for nothing and feared nothing, taking this path to its end brought about a deep sense of serenity and indescribable joy beyond all earthly pleasures. "The Spirit of man" says "The Supreme Teaching," "has crossed the lands of good and evil, and has passed beyond the sorrows of the heart." There would be no rebirth, because there would be no clinging to life, no dread of dying, just a state of equanimity towards the world. This was *moksha*. It was a goal that could be realized in one's lifetime, and those who did were called *jivanmuktas*—living, liberated souls.

Some texts refer to the experience of *moksha* as merging with or returning to Brahman, but those images are a bit misleading. The soul does not need to unite with Brahman because it already *is* Brahman; it merely fails to recognize that. *Moksha*, then, is less an achievement than the simple apprehension of truth. And here we encounter another paradox of this spiritual pathway. Although the jivanmukta must strive to reach liberation, it's not the effort that accomplishes unity with Brahman. This remarkable insight was beautifully expressed by a mystic from another tradition similar in many ways to Vedanta. Bayazid al-Bistami, a medieval Sufi, told his followers: "This thing we tell of can never be found by seeking, yet only seekers find it." So it was with the path of Vedanta.

I've been describing the identity of Brahman and *atman* as a lofty conception, but that doesn't mean as theology it has no problems. For instance, how does one account for *maya*, the veil of illusion over reality? If Brahman-*atman* is the only reality there is, why does the illusion of *maya* exist and how is it created? An even more vexing question is this: if there are no individuals, then there are no souls in the plural. But if there are no souls, only *atman*-Brahman, in what sense is transmigration real? Is *samsara* itself an illusion? In an intriguing passage, one Upanishad comes very close to making this claim. It says, "*Samsara*, the transmigration of life, takes place in one's own mind. Let one therefore keep the mind pure, for what a man thinks that he becomes: this is the mystery of Eternity."

The Upanishads blended tantalizing and provocative ideas with just enough vagueness and uncertainty to inspire successive generations to continue to work through and reinterpret its essential features. No less than three subschools of Hindu philosophy were based on Vedanta, and they each develop different perspectives on the issues that we've been discussing. Two of Hinduism's greatest philosophers, Shankara and Ramanuja, both post-Axial sages, were founders of Vedantin schools.

But the Upanishads' significance goes well beyond providing grist for the philosophers' mill; its importance to the overall Hindu tradition was more a matter of establishing the key elements that provided Hinduism with many of its characteristic features: the belief in the unity and incomprehensible nature of ultimate reality; the conceptions of *samsara*, karma, *atman*, and *moksha*; and the sense that the world and our selves are not really the way they appear.

Despite its profound importance in the Hindu tradition, though, not everyone found the Vedantic perspective congenial to his or her religious sensibilities. As Hinduism evolved through the Axial period, it continued to add new perspectives and practices to accommodate individual beliefs and tastes. Ultimately, Hinduism became a family of religions without a creed or a core of beliefs that every Hindu was expected to accept. Unlike other religions in which doctrinal purity is essential and dissidents are excommunicated, Hinduism has embraced differences rather than excluded them. Early on, Hinduism recognized that people were at different stages in their spiritual lives and that the practices and beliefs for one person might not be suitable for another. This realization has always been one of the most attractive characteristics of Hinduism to me. In its most quoted passage, the Rig Veda declares "Truth is one; but the wise call it by various names." Rather than impose a single set of doctrines and rituals, Hinduism has given wide latitude for persons to appropriate its vast resources in the way most meaningful and enriching for the individual.

As one might expect, many Indians found the Upanishads' path of knowledge simply too demanding and unappealing as a way of life. The mystical tradition of imageless silence may attract some, but by far most religious folk need some symbols and words to guide their spirits. Aristotle wrote, "The soul never thinks without an image," and most people need to think about and conceptualize the object of their devotion. Consequently, most Hindus preferred a more traditional piety that was focused on the worship of a personal god or goddess to the highly abstract, and impersonal Brahman.

That there are no temples in India dedicated to Brahman is evidence that conventional religious practices such as prayer and ceremonies are not conducive to this concept of ultimate reality. I mean, how does one pray to an inconceivable principle? How does one ask for healing or favors from Brahman? How does one celebrate or tell stories about Brahman? The ultimate reality without qualities simply did not satisfy the religious needs of many. But because the emerging Hinduism did not insist on uniformity of practice and belief, this was not really a problem. The worship of personal deities continued unabated in the Axial Age and became even more popular near its end, and afterwards, with the composition of the Bhagavad-Gita, perhaps the most frequently read Hindu scripture.

The historical co-existence of these two paths—one of devotion to the gods and goddesses and the other of seeking realization of Brahman—naturally invites us to ask about the relationship between these two very different religious outlooks. The way of knowledge emphasizes that ultimate reality is inconceivable and beyond words and images, yet anyone who knows much about India knows that Hindus are anything but silent about god. India is a land of an astounding array of divine icons. There are pictures and statues of members of the Hindu pantheon everywhere you go: in the public buildings; on buses; in the taxis and rickshaws; at the tea stalls and shops; on the sides of road. The gods and goddesses cast a watchful eye over everything. The causal observer could hardly guess that the ultimate reality of Hinduism was incomprehensible and beyond image.

To incorporate these vast numbers of anthropomorphic gods and goddesses who are venerated all throughout India, Hinduism refined the theology of Brahman. By introducing another dimension to the theory of Brahman, Hindu theologians provided a way for the devotees of the gods and the seekers of Brahman to understand themselves as relating to the same ultimate reality. And in doing so, Hinduism provided the theoretical foundations for its broad tolerance and inclusive outlook.

The Upanishads clearly emphasize the incomprehensible nature of Brahman; but later thinkers would say there is a sense in which Brahman *is* knowable and can be represented and comprehended, not completely of course, but in a partial manner. Thus, in addition to the claim that Brahman was *nirguna*—a term that means without qualities and beyond the mind's grasp—later theologians argued that Brahman was also *saguna*, with qualities, and therefore able to be conceived and perceived. The formless and the infinite could take form and finitude. On this belief, the many gods and goddesses of popular piety were so many manifestations of the one inconceivable reality. Through devotion to any manifestation, the individual therefore relates to Brahman. Each god or goddess functions as a portal or a conduit to the ultimate reality, mediating the sacred to the believer.

The idea of Saguna Brahman recognizes that most people require a concrete focus for the religious life, a symbol or image towards which they can orient their devotion, and direct their prayers, and grasp something of the nature of the ultimate. Even those on the mystical path to Nirguna Brahman, at some point in their journey needed symbols of the divine, although they now strive to go beyond them. Throughout their history Hindus have fashioned physical representations of its gods and goddesses to provide these centers of faith. Since most Hindus historically—and many still today—cannot read, these physical images are the principal source of their theology.

Hindu images of the divine can be anthropomorphic; that is, human like, or non-anthropomorphic. Since Brahman pervades all there is, in principle anything can manifest divine reality and yield access to the sacred for those who have the eyes to see. The countless array of non-anthropomorphic symbols include things like stones, and trees, rivers, celestial bodies, and other prominent non-anthropomorphic representations are the lingam that symbolizes the presence of Shiva and the footprints of Vishnu.

The anthropomorphic images are those that appear humanlike. To imagine ultimate reality as in some measure like us—with intelligence, will, emotions, and perhaps even a body—helps imagine mystery and to relate to it in ways that are not possible with non-anthropomorphic representations. Anthropomorphic images allow devotees to feel close to the highest reality and believe that whoever or whatever is in charge of this world is concerned about human well-being.

The danger in personalizing the divine, however, is making it seem too human until it appears utterly finite and unworthy of devotion. The recent furor over several fictional accounts of the life of Jesus—*The Last Temptation of Christ*, *The Da Vinci Code*, and Mel Gibson's *The Passion of the Christ*—all concern this very issue. Among other things, critics argue that these stories so strongly emphasize Jesus' humanity that his divinity is virtually lost.

Hindu images of the gods are designed to avert this danger by incorporating elements that bluntly remind devotees that the gods are not like us and cannot be reduced to finite status. The Hindu gods thus appear simultaneously human and nonhuman. Ganesha, the remover of obstacles, has a very human body, but the head of an elephant. Lord Rama, a manifestation of the god Vishnu, appears to be completely human, but his blue skin reminds Hindus of his divinity. The Goddess Durga looks like a woman, but her eight arms tell us she is not. Each of these instances helps give shape to the unseen and allows Hindus to glimpse some salient aspect of the divine. Durga's many arms, for example, indicate immense power, just as Brahma's many heads suggest omniscience. The androgynous image known as Ardhanari is half god Shiva and half goddess Parvati, expressing the ideal of balance between male and female principles. At the same time, the unusual qualities such as multiple arms, or heads, or bisexual bodies remind devotees that the divine always transcends ordinary experience.

These unearthly characteristics serve to point beyond the human-made image to ultimate, infinite reality. As symbols, no one would confuse the images with that to which they refer. Yet there is a special sense in which they are understood to embody the divine reality, allowing the images to function as incarnations of the god.

When it is completed by a craftsperson, the god or goddess the image represents may be invited to inhabit it through elaborate rituals of consecration. In a temple, the consecrated image is then treated as if it were the god in living form. In the morning, it's gently awakened from sleep, bathed and clothed, decorated with flower garlands and cosmetics, and offered food. During the day, the image is given gifts such flowers, fruit, water, and coconuts. At specific times during the day, the temple image is made available to worshipers for *darśan*. *Darśan* is a special viewing of the divine image. Seeing the god and, just as important, being seen by the god is a transaction of great importance in Hinduism. At night, the image is affectionately put to bed.

Ordinarily, the incarnation lasts for a specific period of time, perhaps for a weeklong festival in honor of the *deva*. When the designated term is up, the physical image is destroyed, often by burning or immersion in water, in what amounts to a funeral. This practice reminds devotees that although the god may indeed incarnate the image, the image is not the god. It's still the product of human creation. The image is like an impermanent body, temporarily housing a soul, just as the soul briefly inhabits a human body.

Even though the Hindu pantheon is immense, individual Hindus do not worship all the gods. Each devotee has an *ista-devatā*, a personal deity of choice. Often this personal deva is the god venerated by one's family or village, but it is not uncommon for family members to be devoted to different gods. One's decision to worship a specific god is uniquely one's own, and it may be based on a special affinity that one feels for a particular god. Devotees worship their chosen deity as the supreme god, but they do not feel compelled to deny the reality of the other gods or their supremacy of these gods for their followers. In a land of 330 million gods—and that's the traditional number of the Hindu pantheon—this is how Hindus can understand themselves to be monotheists.

Now, many in the Western world consider the religious use of images blasphemous and accordingly they refer to them as idols. Often those who level such criticism against the use of physical images fail to realize that their own beliefs and theologies are full of images for the divine, albeit linguistic rather than material images. To call god father or king and to carve a statue of Vishnu are both human efforts to give form to that which is ultimately formless. Unless one is absolutely silent about ultimate reality, it not possible to avoid human-made images and concepts. And all human images—physical and linguistic—are subject to the dangers of idolatry. Idolatry is not creating physical symbols or representations of god, as such, but of confusing and identifying transcendent divine reality with what is merely the product of our minds and hands. Idolatry means to believe that god really is a father or that god really has four heads, rather than recognize that these are images and metaphors that we have created merely to help us grasp an elusive mystery.

Here is where Nirguna Brahman is of immense theological value. The idea of Nirguna Brahman reminds the devotee that the ultimate reality always transcends any image. Nirguna Brahman means that no single representation of god or goddess could ever exhaust the limitlessness of Brahman, or for that matter neither could 330 million images. The very number of gods in Hinduism and their complex manifestations, so outrageous in their extravagance, serves to astound and overwhelm the human mind. And that, in a fashion, reminds Hindus of the ultimate reality's unspeakable nature. Thus the Nirguna Brahman provides a safeguard against absolutistic claims about god and promotes what I call epistemological humility, recognition of the limited capacities of the human mind in the face of universal mystery.

The best resource within Hinduism for understanding the dynamics of the gods is probably the Bhagavad-Gita, the popular scripture that was written down at the end of the Axial Age, or just shortly afterwards. Primarily a dialogue between a warrior named Arjuna and the god Krishna, the Gita is a veritable tour through the many practices of Hinduism, including Vedic rituals, karma and morality, meditation and yoga, and devotion to the gods. One of the central points is that all of these disciplines are spiritually beneficial. But the Gita also suggests that devotion to god is the best of all. Towards the end of the book, Krishna encourages Arjuna to focus his mind, will, and heart on god and to let go of all else. And in so doing, Arjuna—and any devotee—will find liberation from *samsara*. Krishna says:

> Whatever you do—whatever you take,
> Whatever you offer, what you give,
> What penances you perform—
> Do as an offering to me…!
>
> And you will be freed from the bonds of [karma],
> From the fruit of fortune and misfortune;
> Armed with the discipline of renunciation,
> Your self liberated, you will join me.

All that matters is to do all things with faith and dedication to the god. According to the Gita, faith can be so potent it does not even matter whether one is devoted to the god Krishna by name.

> When devoted men sacrifice
> To other deities with faith,
> They sacrifice to me…,
> However aberrant the rites.

What matters is not the object of faith but its quality and sincerity.

Well, we have observed two fundamentally different theologies and practices emerging in the Indian Axial Age: The first, a mystical theology in which ultimate reality is beyond the reach of the mind; and the second, a theistic view in which the divine can represented by symbols and images, allowing the devotee to draw close through acts of reverence and veneration. While followers of both paths may claim superiority for his or her particular way, both approaches have been embraced by the greater tradition of Hinduism. Neither can claim to be more authentically Hindu than the other.

This brings to a close our extremely brief look at the emergence of Hinduism in the Axial Age. In our next conversation, we'll begin to explore another perspective that begins in the ferment of Northern India and develops into the religion that takes it name from perhaps India's greatest sage, the Buddha.

Lecture Eleven
The Life of Siddhattha Gotama

Scope:

Among the many seekers of liberation in the South Asian Axial Age was a man whose given name was Siddhattha Gotama. Prompted by a shocking encounter with sickness, old age, and death, Gotama became one of the thousands of renouncers in northeastern India seeking relief from the endless suffering of *samsara*. With attention to both the historically verifiable and the mythic aspects of his biography, this lecture traces Gotama's life from his birth into privileged circumstances through his practice of extreme asceticism and, finally, to his determination to seek liberation by the Middle Way.

Outline

I. Siddhattha Gotama was among the thousands of intrepid individuals who sought to end *samsara* in northeastern India during the Axial Age, the figure who eventually became known as the Buddha. We begin with some accepted historical knowledge about his early life, distinguishing the historical Buddha from later embellishments of his life.

A. The earliest Buddhist scriptures existed in oral tradition and were not written down until 300–400 years after his death. As the tradition developed and spread, new scriptures were added, and views of the Buddha's life and significance also changed.

B. The Pali Canon, the Buddhist texts closest in time to his life, is the most reliable source for constructing his life. For our purposes, the most important part of the canon is the set of writings called the *Suttas*, or discourses, which the Buddhist tradition considers the direct words of the Buddha himself.

C. The Pali Suttas say little about the Buddha's life before his awakening; thus, we can construct only an outline of his life using these scriptures.

D. We know that there was an individual named Gotama who was born into a privileged life in the area near the current border between India and Nepal. Though there is debate on the actual dates, according to tradition, he was born in 563 B.C.E., well within the Axial Age. (The majority of scholars today place his date of birth near 490 B.C.E.)

E. Historical scholarship tells us that Gotama underwent a profound, life-changing experience that eventually led him to new insights into the human condition and to a new spiritual movement. He taught his ideas to a growing body of followers throughout northeastern India during the period of great social change and religious ferment.

F. Following his awakening, the Buddha's teaching ministry lasted for several decades until he died. Tradition says that he lived until the age of 80.

II. Little else can be said about the historical Buddha with much certainty, but there are several versions of his early life and how he came to claim the title *the Buddha*. Most of them are variations on a basic storyline, as follows.

A. Though modern historiography places doubt on this royal lineage, Siddhattha was born to the king and queen of the Sakyan peoples. Although it is true that Siddhattha's family was privileged, it is unlikely that his parents were monarchs, because the small states of this area were tribal republics ruled by councils of elders.

B. One late addition to the narrative suggests that Siddhattha was conceived by his mother, Queen Maya, during a dream in which she was impregnated by a god-like King Elephant, a divinely ordained and supernaturally accomplished conception.

1. Ten months later, the child Siddhattha was born, while his mother was on a journey to the home of her parents.
2. He sprung from his mother's side while she stood upright, holding the branch of a tree.
3. Immediately, the newborn took seven steps and confidently declared that he was born for the good of the world and this would be his last birth in the samsaric realm.

C. Other versions of Siddhattha's birth include his father's consultation with court astrologers, who agreed that the child would become a *cakravartin*, a "wheel-turner," one whose existence would decisively change the lives of others. Whether or not he would become a great monarch or forsake the world and follow the path of the spiritual pioneer was unclear to the astrologers.

D. Determined that his son become a monarch like himself, Siddhattha's father was advised to shield his son from unpleasantness and raise him in a wholly delightful environment, with the best food, the best clothes, and the best entertainment. He couldn't be exposed to the brutal realities of existence until he firmly committed himself to being king.

E. Some say Siddhattha wasn't allowed to leave the palace; others suggest that he made occasional excursions, but only after his father had arranged to have Siddhattha's route purged of potentially upsetting sights. Beggars, elderly people, and the sick and disabled were kept off the streets.

F. At 16, Siddhattha married his beautiful cousin Yashodhara, who eventually gave birth to his son. Everything seemed right with the world. And so it was, for Siddhattha's first 29 years.

G. Whether historical or not, the story of Siddhattha's early life suggests that without even working for it, he already had everything other people spend their lives pursuing: riches, power, celebrity, and every imaginable creature comfort.

III. Though young Siddhattha epitomized the fulfillment of humanity's greatest dreams, having it all was still not enough. At the age of 29, he realized this insight after coming face-to-face with suffering for the first time.

A. Siddhattha encountered a person in the throes of illness, another ravaged by age, and a corpse en route to the charnel ground. Up until that moment, he had never witnessed or heard of any of these things.

B. Siddhattha was distressed to learn about the realities of life and to discover that all beings were subject to old age, illness, and death.

C. At the same time, he also encountered a wandering *samana* who had renounced everything but nonetheless appeared happy in the midst of a suffering world.

D. Distraught by the first three spectacles and intrigued by the fourth, Siddhattha decided to give up the comforts of the privileged life to seek a way to soothe his now troubled mind. The Buddhist traditions refer to this episode as the "Four Sights."

E. Siddhattha left his family and home forever, taking up the life of a *samana*.

F. Some elements of this story seem preposterous; for example, could he really have been sheltered from life's harsh realities or been oblivious to suffering, old age, and death for nearly 30 years?

   1. It's possible that Siddhattha's real epiphany, significantly occurring at the age when the lives of Jesus, Zoroaster, Ezekiel, Mahavira, and Guru Nanak also took dramatic turns, came when he recognized that he himself was subject to the realities of life.

   2. At this critical moment, Siddhattha's illusion was shattered, and there was simply no returning to a life that ignored suffering and death.

G. Rather than serenity, Siddhattha's first epiphany brought profound agitation. It meant dropping the pretense of uniqueness and accepting wholeheartedly one's common share with everyone else.

IV. Siddhattha traveled throughout the cities of the Ganges basin, a novice *samana* in search of ascetics who could teach him the disciplines that would end his *samsara*.

A. His first teacher was a renowned master of yogic meditation. After mastering this doctrine and reaching a state of "nothingness," however, Siddhattha found that it did not bring him freedom.

B. Under the tutelage of his second instructor, Siddhattha was able to reach the level of "neither perception nor non-perception," but this, too, failed to provide the wisdom he sought.

C. These practices brought extraordinary—but only temporary—experiences. Siddhattha wanted to attain permanent freedom from suffering and *samsara.* He continued to find value in meditation, but he rejected his teachers' claims that their states of meditation were the highest realization of the spiritual life.

D. Siddhattha then practiced self-mortification, depriving himself of food until he became emaciated. He concluded that far from terminating suffering, this practice only intensified it. Surely, there had to be some other way to conquer *samsara*.

Essential Reading:

Carrithers, *Buddha*, chapters 1–3.

Supplementary Reading:

Ñanamoli, *The Life of the Buddha*, chapters 1–2.

Questions to Consider:

1. Why might the myth of Siddhattha's life be just as important as factual information in understanding what came to be known as Buddhism?
2. What is significant about the age at which Siddhattha had his first epiphany?

Lecture Eleven—Transcript
The Life of Siddhattha Gotama

Among the thousands of intrepid individuals who sought to end samsara—the transmigration of life—in the forests of northeastern India in the Axial Age was a young man by the name of Siddhattha Gotama. Like many others, Gotama had been convinced that the conquering of the anguish of samsaric existence was life's highest aspiration. Nothing else could be more important. And, like many others, he was willing to give up everything to attain that goal. Yet, his pursuit of the spiritual options available to him at that time brought him no satisfaction. He quickly mastered the ascetic disciplines for realizing Brahman but found that they did not bring what he was looking for. The way of devotion to the gods held little interest for him; he thought the gods themselves were in need of the solutions he sought. After many years of frustration, he departed these well-trodden paths and on his own discovered the object of his search. His discovery finally brought him happiness and relief from the suffering that appeared to be inherent to life itself. Siddhattha Gotama had become *the Buddha.*

Today, we'll begin our study of this remarkable individual, with special attention to his early experiences that led him to discover a new perspective that became one of the world's great religions. In later lectures, we'll look at the teachings and practices he espoused and compare them to other Axial Age philosophies that we've already examined. For the first time in our study of the Indian Axial Age, we have an actual historical individual to whom we can connect specific teachings. It's important to study the Buddha's teachings in the context of his life because the two are so closely intertwined. The Buddha was not an armchair philosopher; his view was the direct result of his attentive engagement with his own experience, a habit of being that he encouraged in his followers.

Like other founders of religious movements, we can distinguish the historical Buddha from the Buddha of myth and history. By the historical Buddha, I mean the actual individual who lived in human history and what we can say about him with reasonable certainty, using modern methods of historiography. By the Buddha of myth and legend, I mean the aspects of his life that are later embellishments added by his followers after his death. In many cases, the line between history and myth is not always easy to draw, and scholars constantly debate what belongs on one side or the other.

Part of the difficulty in recovering the historical Buddha resides in the nature of our sources. The earliest Buddhist scriptures existed in oral tradition and were not written down until 300–400 years after the Buddha's death. Furthermore, as the Buddhist tradition continued to develop and spread to different regions of Asia, new scriptures were added to reflect the philosophical emphases of the emerging new sects. As Buddhism evolved, followers' views of the Buddha's life and its significance also changed.

The Pali Canon, the Buddhist texts closest in time to the life of the Buddha, are the most reliable sources for constructing the life of the historical Buddha. There are also collections of scriptures in Tibetan, Sanskrit, and Chinese, which were written later and are less historically dependable than the Pali Canon. Pali, by the way, refers to the language of the texts. The Buddha probably did not speak Pali himself but a Sanskritic language close to it. Pali is also a Sanskritic language, not the formal Sanskrit used by the Brahmin priests, but a vernacular spoken by ordinary people. The Pali collection comprises a large number of volumes, enough to occupy an entire library shelf. The most important part of the canon for our purposes is the set of writings called the *Suttas*, or discourses, which the Buddhist tradition considers to be the direct words of the Buddha himself.

Interestingly, the Pali Suttas tell us very little about the Buddha's life prior to his awakening experience. The clear focus of these writings is his teachings. If we adhere to the modern standards of historical scholarship, we can only set forth a bare-bones outline of his life using these scriptures.

Based on those standards, we can say with fairly high confidence that there was in fact an individual named Gotama who was born into privileged circumstances in the area near the current border between India and Nepal. At this time, the area was occupied by Indo-Aryans known the *Shakyas*. According to traditions based on the Pali texts, Gotama was born in the year 563 B.C.E. As with Zoroaster, scholars are not in complete agreement about when Gotama actually lived, but the range of dates are not nearly as widespread as that of Zoroaster's. The majority of scholars today would place his date of birth near 490 B.C.E. In any event, the Indian sage lived well within the Axial Age.

Historical scholarship also tells us that Gotama underwent a profound life-changing experience near the age of 30 that eventually led him to new insights into the human condition and to a new spiritual movement based on his discoveries. He taught his ideas to a growing body of followers throughout northeastern India during the period of great social change and religious ferment. There is good reason to believe that the Suttas of the Pali Canon accurately reflect the essential core of his teaching, although almost certainly some ideas of later interpreters have been included. Following his awakening, the Buddha's teaching ministry lasted for several decades until he died. Tradition says that he lived until the age of 80.

Beyond these sparse statements, little else can be said about the historical Buddha with much certainty. But this meager outline leaves so much out of the Buddha's life story that has provided inspiration and meaning to Buddhists for over two millennia. For this reason, we must risk leaving the historically verifiable facts and venture into the realm of myth and legend. But it is precisely in this realm that we ascertain so much of what made the Buddha such a compelling figure for millions. The life of the Buddha as told in these traditions—whether historically true or not—is the very embodiment of Buddhist teachings, so we dare not neglect the legendary literature.

There are several versions of the early life of Gotama and how he came to claim the title the Buddha. Most of them are variations on a basic story line that runs like this. Siddhattha Gotama was born to the king and queen of the realm of the Sakyan peoples. Modern historiography, though, places doubt on this royal lineage. While it is true that Gotama's family was privileged and members of the warrior caste, it's unlikely that his parents were monarchs, since the small states of this area were tribal republics ruled by councils of elders. But again, to remain strictly on the side of history eliminates the deeper significance of the story. One late addition to the narrative suggests that Siddhattha was conceived by his mother Queen Maya during a dream in which she was impregnated by a white god-like king elephant, implying that his conception was divinely ordained and supernaturally accomplished. This variation goes on to say that ten months later the child Siddhattha was born while his mother was on a journey to the home of her parents. Along the way, she gave birth in a grove of trees near the town of Lumbini. The child came forth from his mother's side while she stood upright, holding the branch of a tree. Immediately, the newborn took seven steps and confidently declared that he was born for the good of the world and that this would be his last birth in the samsaric realm. Clearly, this tale is mythic, but it serves to foreground the universal significance of Siddhattha's life.

Not all versions include this miraculous birth story, but most of them contain the account of Prince Siddhattha's father's consultation with his court astrologers after his son's birth. The soothsayers all agreed: the king's first-born would become a *cakravartin*, a wheel-turner, one whose existence would decisively change the lives of others. But the court sages were not clear about the specific domain of Siddhattha's accomplishments. He might pursue the way of the world and become a great monarch. Or he might forsake the world and follow the path of the spiritual pioneer. Determined to see his son follow in his own footsteps, King Suddhodana asked how he might ensure that his son take the road to kingship. Again, the court sages were unanimous: at all costs, the boy must be shielded from any unpleasantness and raised in a wholly delightful environment. He must enjoy only the best food, wear the best clothes, and engage in constant diversions and entertainments. He must never be exposed to the brutal realities of existence until he had firmly committed himself to being king.

Suddhodana followed the sages' recommendations zealously and to the letter. The accounts offer various and differing details. Some say Siddhattha was never permitted to leave the palace; others suggest that he made occasional excursions beyond the palace confines, but only after his father had arranged to have the young man's route carefully planned and purged of potentially upsetting sights. Beggars, old men and women, sick and disabled were all rounded up and kept out of sight until the prince's entourage had passed. By all accounts, Siddhattha lived only the most pleasant sort of life, unaware of that there was any other way to live. In a rare self-revelation in the Pali Canon, the Buddha described his early years in a way that confirms the essence of the legend although it doesn't confirm all the details. Many years after his awakening, the Buddha tells his followers:

> I was delicate, most delicate, supremely delicate. Lily pools were made for me at my father's house solely for my benefit.

> Blue lilies flowered in one, white lilies in another, red lilies in a third. I used no sandalwood that was not from [the city of] Benares. My turban, tunic, lower garments and cloak were all made of Benares cloth. A white sunshade was held over me day and night so that no cold or heat or dust or grit or dew might inconvenience me.

At age 16, Siddhattha married his beautiful cousin, Yashodhara, who eventually gave birth to his son. Everything seemed right with the world. And so it was, for Siddhattha's first 29 years.

Again, whether historical or not, the story of his father's royal status, wealth, power, and overprotectiveness is rich with meaning. It suggests that without even lifting a finger, the individual who would become the Buddha had already received everything other people spend their entire lives trying to get. Simply by virtue of birth, he had riches, power, celebrity, every imaginable creature comfort. Even according to the Pali accounts, Siddhattha was uncommonly handsome with deep blue eyes, athletically endowed, blessed with robust health, and the love of family, and a deeply compassionate nature. It's hard even to imagine what more could be added to such a life. This young Gotama epitomized the fulfillment of humanity's greatest dreams, the embodiment of what almost all of us think we want. But this is the very point of the legend of Siddhattha's extravagant early life: Having it all is still not enough.

In a crucial moment, at the age of 29, whether by accident or design (and various texts say various things), the shell of his sheltered existence was cracked, and Siddhattha came face-to-face with suffering for the very first time. In short order, he encountered a person in the throes of illness, another ravaged by age, and a corpse en route to the charnel ground. The narrative claims that, up until that moment, the prince had never witnessed any of these things or had even heard of sickness, old age, and death. Learning about these realities of life and discovering that all beings were subject to them caused Siddhattha great distress. On his return home, he saw another impressive sight: a wandering *samana* who had renounced everything and who nonetheless appeared happy in the midst of a suffering world. Distraught by the first three spectacles and intrigued by the fourth, the young man decided to give up the comforts of the privileged life to seek a way to soothe his now troubled mind. The Buddhist traditions refer to this episode as the "Four Sights."

Siddhattha took immediate action. In the dark of night, he quietly kissed his wife and young son goodbye and left palace life forever. With the help of his close friend, he slipped out of his father's house, cut off his hair, and took up the robes and begging bowl of the *samanas*.

There is quite a bit in this story that makes it hard to accept as historically true, which is why most scholars assign it to the category of myth. It's hard to believe that as zealous as his father was to shield Siddhattha's life from life's harsh realities, that he could have actually pulled it off for three decades. It's equally difficult to think that for so many years the young man was totally oblivious to suffering, old age, and death. I think the legend needs a touch of demythologizing to uncover its real depth.

Rather than the story of a father's overprotectiveness, I propose that the account is really about youthful naïveté. While I believe that something of great significance happened to Siddhattha at 29, I seriously doubt it was learning that people get sick, get old, and die. I think he knew these things already. The real epiphany for Siddhattha came when he recognized that he himself, the one who had it all, as well as everyone he cared about, were all subject to these realities of life. Prior to this moment, Siddhattha's knowledge of these truths was merely abstract and conceptual. We all know from a fairly young age that living things die: as a kid, I squashed too many bugs and saw too many dead armadillos on Texas roadsides to be oblivious to death. What I was unaware of—or what I sometimes consciously denied (and I have clear recollections of this)—was that death would happen to me. For much of our lives, especially in our youth, we don't really believe death will come to us.

Leo Tolstoy's novella, *The Death of Ivan Ilyich*, is a disturbing study of the psychological mechanisms for preventing our personal demise from coming to full consciousness. When word of Ivan Ilyich's death reaches his associates, his close friend Pyotr Ivanovich momentarily lets the news upset him and then quickly, but only half-consciously, reasons it away:

> Pyotr Ivanovich was overcome with horror as he thought of the suffering of someone he had known so well, first as a carefree boy, then as a schoolmate, later as a grown man, his colleague.... "Three days of terrible suffering and death. Why, the same thing could happen to me at anytime now,"

> he thought and for a moment he felt panic-stricken. But at once, he himself did not know how, he was rescued by the customary reflection that all this happened to Ivan Ilyich, not to him, that it could not and should not happen to him; and that if he were to grant such a possibility, he would succumb to depression…. With this line of reasoning, Pyotr Ivanovich set his mind at rest and began to press for details about Ivan Ilyich's death, as though death were a chance experience that could only happen to Ivan Ilyich, never to himself.

The kind of forgetfulness that overcame Pyotr Ivanovich like a narcotic was not possible for Siddhattha Gotama. At this critical moment, Siddhattha truly got it: "I, too, will die; I will lose everything I hold dear." His illusion had shattered, and there was simply no way of returning to life as if suffering and death were not real.

Significantly, this insight comes to Siddhattha near the time that he is of the age of 30; the same age when the lives of Jesus, Zoroaster, Ezekiel, Mahavira, and Guru Nanak took dramatic turns. Why 30? I can only offer some speculation based largely on my own experience. It was at thirty that I became personally acquainted with the aging of my body, and I suspect that this begins to happen to others around this age. I began to see little signs that my youth was becoming a thing of the past—a tiny wrinkle here, a little sagging there, more hair in the shower drain. It wasn't much that anyone else could detect, but to someone as self-centered as me, these things caused me much anxiety. It took me a long time to come to terms with this fact of life. I simply did not believe these things were happening to me; like Pyotr Ivanovich, I assumed that an exception would be made in my case.

With these reflections, I am suggesting that one way to read the story of the "Four Sights" is as Siddhattha's complete acceptance that aging and death would indeed come to him, and not just to others. It hardly matters whether Siddhattha grasped this by stealthily observing his father's kingdom, or by looking in the mirror, or just calmly contemplating the natural course of life. In whatever way it happened, this recognition—I believe—was the Buddha's first awakening, his first enlightenment. Without this experience, there would have been no second awakening, no illumination while quietly sitting under a tree several years later. Unlike his subsequent and ultimate awakening, this first epiphany brought not serenity of mind, but profound agitation and restiveness. It meant dropping the pretense of uniqueness and accepting wholeheartedly one's common share with everyone else. It was enough to cause him to walk away from his incomparable life of ease and comfort. Presumably, he may have stayed right within his walls of pleasure. He might have done what most of us do when the recognition of our frailties come upon us: that is, denying and forgetting. We are constantly seeking new ways to put our vulnerabilities out of mind. As T. S. Eliot once said, "Humankind cannot bear very much reality." But for the young Gotama, returning to naïveté was not an option. Reality was just too real.

So he left and took up the homeless life of the wandering ascetic, like so many others had done. From his home in the Himalayan foothills he traveled on foot towards the urban centers of the Ganges basin and spent the rest of his life in this rapidly developing region. As a novice *samana*, Gotama sought someone who could serve as a teacher, introducing him to the disciplines to find the end to suffering and rebirth. His first teacher was Alara Kalama, a renowned master of yogic meditation. Gotama soon mastered his teacher's doctrine and the meditative states on which they were based. Alara Kalama's instruction was able to take the aspiring *samana* to the state of what he called nothingness, but no further. Siddhattha found that this state did not bring him the freedom that he sought, and he left in search of someone else who could take him further. His second instructor, Uddaka Ramaputta, was also a famous practitioner of meditative yoga. Under his tutelage, Siddhattha was able reach the level of "neither perception nor nonperception," but he also knew that this meditative state did not provide the wisdom he was looking for. So he left Ramaputta. These practices brought extraordinary—but only temporary—experiences. As long as he was absorbed in meditation, Siddhattha's experience was quite pleasant, but after the meditation ended, so did the pleasant state. Siddhattha wanted to attain permanent freedom from suffering and samsara. He continued to find value in meditation, but he rejected his teachers' claims that their states of meditation were the highest realization of the spiritual life.

The young *samana* next took his quest to a more extreme level, involving self-mortification. When he took up the practice of intense asceticism, Siddhattha did so with the same zeal that had characterized his work with his yoga teachers. He deprived his body of food and subsisted on a paltry diet of rice or beans. In the Pali Canon, he describes his appearance after many months of this kind of self-torture:

> My body reached a state of extreme emaciation. Because of eating so little my limbs became like the jointed segments of vine stems or bamboo stems...my backside became like a camel's hoof... the projections on my spine stood forth like corded beads...my ribs jutted out as gaunt as the crazy rafters on a roofless barn...the gleam of my eyes sank far down in their sockets...my belly skin adhered to my backbone; thus if I touched my belly skin I encountered my backbone.

To passers-by, the contemplative ascetic looked like a decaying corpse.

Gotama was so dedicated to his task and committed to this discipline that a small group of five disciples gathered around him, hoping to follow him on his path. But eventually, Gotama concluded that this way was literally a dead-end. Far from terminating suffering, self-mortification only intensified it and its ultimate destination could only be death. Surely there had to be some other way to conquering *samsara*.

Lecture Twelve
"I Am Awake"

Scope:

As a consequence of a profound enlightenment experience at age 35, Siddhattha Gotama claims the title *the Buddha*, the "Awakened One." Based on the insights of this experience, the Buddha inaugurated a 45-year ministry of teaching to renouncers and householders alike. In this and the next two lectures, we explore the substance of his Dhamma, or teaching, as expressed principally through the Four Noble Truths. The first of these principles concerns the nature of suffering. The Buddha's understanding of suffering was deep and subtle and, hence, requires careful explanation lest his entire teaching, which is based on this idea, be misunderstood. This lecture looks at how the Buddha could see suffering as a pervasive and insidious mark of all existence, even though life manifests moments of pleasure and happiness.

Outline

I. Siddhattha Gotama fervently practiced the contemplative and ascetic arts for six years after renouncing his former privileged lifestyle. Yet he realized that neither pleasure and delight nor self-denial and mortification would bring him the peace he sought. Setting a course between the two extremes, he devised an approach called the *Middle Way*.

- **A.** Once he decided to find this Middle Way, Siddhattha began caring for his ravaged body; physical well-being would be necessary to pursue liberation.
- **B.** He meditated beneath a tree near the village of Gaya, recalling how he had once paid close attention to his breath, which had brought him a heightened sense of awareness and a pervasive calmness.
- **C.** This type of meditation differed from the practices of his former teachers because it emphasized mindfulness, making one attentive to what was happening in the mind, body, and external environment without judgment. As a result of mindful meditation, the Buddha believed that the mind

would become more receptive to the true nature of the world and the self.

D. According to Buddhist tradition, Siddhattha sat beneath a huge tree—later known as the Bodhi, or "wisdom," tree—and vowed not to leave until he had realized the liberating knowledge that he had sought for so many years.

E. His period of contemplation took him deeper than he had ever gone before. But far more important were the deeper insights into the human condition that he attained, the liberating knowledge he sought.

F. As he advanced toward the goal, he was approached by Mara, the demonic tempter, who tried to lure Siddhattha away by offering him the pleasures of the world and taunting him with threats and doubts.

G. Finally, Siddhattha won the understanding that liberated and conquered *samsara*. He also realized that he would never be reborn into this world again. At this moment, he earned the title *the Buddha*, or the "Awakened One."

II. For 49 days, the Buddha enjoyed his liberation and decided to teach his insights to others. He traveled the region talking to ascetics and anyone who would listen.

A. He first thought of his two teachers but discovered that they had died. Next, he approached his former disciples, five ascetics who had chided him earlier for giving up the ascetic path. When they saw their former mentor, they were astounded by his demeanor and recognized that something profoundly significant had happened to him.

B. The Buddha talked about his insights, laying out what he called the *Four Noble Truths*. The talk is sometimes called the Buddha's "First Discourse" and "Turning the Wheel of Dhamma." The Pali word *Dhamma* might be translated simply as "the truth that leads to liberation."

C. The Four Noble Truths are considered the essence of Buddhism. Most of the Buddha's subsequent teachings might be thought of as explanations and amplifications of these basic points.

D. The Buddha never expected his teachings to be accepted on his authority and, in fact, discouraged such acceptance. He rejected many of the common reasons people find for accepting religious beliefs; instead, he encouraged individuals to take responsibility for their own convictions. His teachings included the following caveats:

1. Do not accept anything simply because it is said to be revelation, or because it comes from sacred texts, or because it is traditional.
2. Do not accept hearsay, or anything on the grounds of pure logic, or because it seems rational.
3. Do not accept anything because you agree after reflecting on it, or because the teacher is competent, or simply because he is regarded as a teacher.

E. The Buddha did not mean, however, that one should accept viewpoints based only on gut feelings, or even if they agreed with one's conscience or reasoning. He believed that reasoning was no more reliable than judgments based on texts or spoken by charismatic individuals.

1. According to the Buddha, a belief should be tested by its results when put into practice.
2. To guard against the possibility of bias or limitations in understanding, acceptable views should be checked against the experience of those who are wise.

III. In his discourse, the Buddha declares the first of his Noble Truths, setting out the primary basis for his worldview. The other three Noble Truths will be discussed in subsequent lectures.

A. The First Noble Truth is that life itself is suffering. All that we experience—birth, aging, illness, and death—is suffering, as are the presence of displeasing things and the absence of pleasing things. Not getting what one wants is also suffering.

B. The word *suffering* was translated from the Pali term *dukkha*, though scholars believe it does not effectively convey what the Buddha meant by *dukkha*.

C. There is "ordinary" *dukkha*, the suffering that accompanies injury, sickness, old age, and death. Then there is the *dukkha* of change, or suffering caused by loss or associated with unpleasantness.

D. The world is in constant flux, creating a state of impermanence, or *anicca*. Though impermanence doesn't cause *dukkha*, one's unwise or unskilled response to the world of change does.

E. When the Buddha referred to *dukkha*, he was describing the fundamental quality of the whole of existence, not merely saying that life had moments of tragedy and sorrow. He suggested that human existence is entangled in *dukkha*.

F. If *dukkha* is comprehensive and constant, it becomes clear that understanding *dukkha* is not just a problem of translation; it is also an experiential issue.

G. What makes *dukkha* a Noble Truth is that we do not fully appreciate the extent to which we suffer or feel the dissatisfaction of existence. Thus, individuals are challenged to discover the depth and breadth of *dukkha* through introspection and observation. The true depth of suffering can be seen only from the perspective of the enlightened mind.

H. *Dukkha* might also refer to disappointment, a pervasive feature of life.

  1. Disappointment and *dukkha* are both the consequence of our own habits of mind. Disappointment is the result of reality not conforming to our expectations.

  2. It is more truthful to say that our desires and expectations do not conform to reality, causing suffering. When the Buddha characterized *dukkha* as not getting what we want, he implicitly put the onus on us, not the thing we want or don't want.

I. The Buddha also states that getting what we want causes disappointment; therefore, both the frustration of desire and the fulfillment of desire contribute to suffering.

J. The problem with achieving our desires is that doing so does not really satisfy us in the way we had hoped. We end up wanting more in order to attain the satisfaction we lack.

K. Desire itself has basic causes that urge us to crave things. In the Second Noble Truth, the Buddha explains the factors that lead us to desire in the first place.

Essential Reading:

Rahula, *What the Buddha Taught*, chapters 1–2.

Supplementary Reading:

Ñanamoli, *The Life of the Buddha*, chapters 1–2.

Questions to Consider:

1. What were the qualities of the Buddha's Middle Way?
2. What are the difficulties with translating the Pali term *dukkha* into English? In what ways might this problem reflect the obstacles an observer has in understanding another religion?

Lecture Twelve—Transcript
"I Am Awake"

For six years following his departure from palace life, Siddhattha Gotama fervently practiced the contemplative and ascetic arts. At last, he concluded that he was no closer to liberation than when he began. It occurred to him that all his life he had been an extremist. As a youth in his father's house, he knew nothing but pleasure and delight. Following his renunciation of that, he knew nothing but self-denial and mortification. He now realized that neither extreme was the path to what he sought, and he surmised that steering a course between them, avoiding the pitfalls of both, was a promising approach. He called this "The Middle Way" and he decided to follow it.

Shortly after making this decision, he went to a nearby river, washed off the dust that had accumulated on his body for many months. A local village girl gave him a bowl of milk rice to eat. With this new approach, he would have to care for his body, and not as an end in itself of course, but because physical well-being was necessary to pursue liberation. The harsh forms of self-mortification had to be relinquished. Gradually, he returned to health. When his five students witnessed this change, they concluded that he was simply not up to the demands of the ascetic life and so they left, as he had left his teachers years before.

A short time later, as he sat beneath a tree near the village of Gaya in the present Indian state of Bihar, Gotama began to contemplate his next steps. Resting in the shade of the tree revived an old memory of sitting under a rose-apple tree as a child, during a Sakyan agricultural festival. He recalled that his father was engaged in ceremonial plowing, and he became bored and restless and, with nothing else to do, began to pay close attention to his breath. In those moments, he discovered a heightened sense of awareness and a pervasive calm that dissolved his boredom and restlessness. Remembering that time, Gotama thought that this gentle practice of meditation might provide the wisdom he was looking for.

What distinguished this form of meditation from the practices of his teachers was its emphasis on the quality of mindfulness. Whereas the goal of other meditations was to become absorbed in extraordinary states of mind, mindfulness meditation aimed at reaching a sharpened awareness of the immediate moment so that one became attentive to what was happening in the mind, the body, and the external environment and witnessing these processes without judgment. Without trying to force particular states of mind, the mindfulness meditator simply observed without controlling. By letting go of goals and releasing preconceptions and judgments, the Buddha believed the mind would become more receptive to insight into the nature of the world and the self.

Buddhist tradition says that on the evening of the full moon in the month of Vesakha (which is between April and May, according to Western calendars), Siddhattha Gotama sat beneath a huge tree and vowed not to leave the spot until he realized the liberating knowledge that he had sought for so many years. He said: "Let only my skin, sinew, and bones remain, let the flesh and blood dry up in my body, but I will not give up this seat without completely attaining awakening."

The species of the tree later became known as the Bodhi or wisdom tree. Its Latin name is *ficus religiosus* (sic *ficus religiosa*). We haven't the time to pursue it in this series, but the frequent appearance of the sacred tree across cultures makes for a very fascinating study. I briefly mentioned the significance of trees in the Indo-Iranian religion, and I'm sure you can think of others. The tree of the knowledge of good and evil in the Garden of Eden, for instance, or the cross on which Jesus died. Those might come to mind. Like the rivers and streams we noted before, important sacred events often occur in or under trees. In part, this significance derives from the tree's morphology: its deep roots and rising trunks and branches connect the underworld, the earth, and the heavens, making it an ideal location for encountering the sacred.

During this month of Vesakha, Gotama began his meditation. In the course of the night, his contemplations took him deeper than he had ever been before. A tradition says that he was even able to recall over 100,000 of his previous lives. But far more important was the deeper insights into the human condition that he attained. This was the liberating knowledge that he was searching for. As he approached the goal, he encountered *Mara*, a demonic tempter, who tried to lure Siddhattha away from his objective by offering him the pleasures of the world and taunting him with threats and doubts, much as Satan tried to do to Jesus in the New Testament. But

Gotama was undeterred. At dawn, as the morning star first appeared in the sky, he knew he had won the understanding that liberates and conquers *samsara*. He later tells his followers that in that instant "the knowledge and the vision arose in me: 'Unshakeable is the liberation of my mind. This is my last birth. Now there is no more re-becoming'." At this moment—and not before—Gotama earns the title, *the Buddha*, which means "the awakened one."

Well, what next? What does one do after attaining permanent, unconditional happiness? For 49 days, the Buddha enjoys his liberation and ponders whether it would be worthwhile to try to teach his insights to others. Could others realize the truths that he saw? He ultimately concluded that while not everyone would understand, many would be receptive and might benefit from his new awareness. He decided to begin with his two teachers, but discovered that they had recently died. He next thought of his former disciples, the five who had ridiculed him for giving up the ascetic path. He traveled on foot to the holy city of Banaras, the most sacred city in India, to see if he could find them, and he learned that they were staying at the nearby Deer Park, a refuge for *samanas*. The Buddha exuded such serenity and happiness, that on the way he was accosted by an individual who wanted to know whether he was a god. The Buddha said "I am no god; I am awake."

When the five ascetics saw their former mentor approaching, they too were astounded by his demeanor and recognized that something of profound significance had transpired in him. His calm appearance melted the resentment that they felt for him, and they welcomed him into their company and invited him to speak. The Buddha's formal talk consisted of a concise formulation of the insights that he had received under the Bodhi tree. This speech contained what the Buddhist tradition calls the Four Noble Truths. The talk is sometimes called the Buddha's First Discourse and Turning the Wheel of Dhamma. The Pali word *Dhamma*, or the Sanskrit word *Dharma* in the Buddhist sense, refers to the Buddha's teachings. It might simply be translated as the truth that leads to liberation.

The Four Noble Truths are considered by many to be the essence of Buddhism. Most of the Buddha's subsequent teachings might be thought of as explanations or amplifications of these basic points. As recorded in the Pali Canon, his first discourse seems rather terse for those unfamiliar with his ideas. As I discuss these teachings, I'll use the Four Noble Truths as a basic framework for convenience, but I'll also draw upon other locations in the Pali scripture to help clarify and assist in helping us understand the Buddha's insights. The Buddha was a masterful teacher and he was skilled in addressing his audiences in ways that suited their intellectual capacities and temperaments, so drawing upon these later teachings will help enrich our understanding of the fundamental principles.

The Buddha never expected his teachings to be accepted on his authority. In fact, he positively discouraged it. In his travels, the Buddha once came to a community of people who were known as the Kalamas, who were confused about what or whom to believe in this age of innumerable gurus and doctrines. The Buddha advised the Kalamas on how to assess the many teachings that they were encountering. He told them:

> Do not accept anything simply because it is said to be revelation;
>
> Do not accept it merely because it is traditional;
>
> Do not accept anything that is hearsay;
>
> Do not accept it because it comes from sacred texts;
>
> Do not accept it only on the grounds of pure logic or because it seems rational;
>
> Do not accept it because you agree with it after reflecting on it;
>
> Do not accept it on the grounds that the teacher is competent or simply because he is regarded as "our teacher";
>
> But when you know *for yourselves* that these things are wholesome; that these things are blameless; that these things are praised by the wise; and that these things, if undertaken and practiced, lead to benefit and happiness, then you should accept them and abide in them.

This advice has a very modern tone to it. It concisely characterizes the Buddha's ideal for practicing his teachings. It encourages the individual to take responsibility for their own convictions and rejects many of the common reasons that people accept religious beliefs.

But the Buddha's advice is misunderstood if it's taken as an endorsement of mere subjectivity, of accepting something as right or wrong on the basis of a gut feeling, or even if it accords with one's conscience or reasoning faculty. You might be surprised to hear the Buddha rejecting pure logic and reasoning as sufficient grounds for accepting a viewpoint. But he believes that reasoning may be no more reliable than judgments based on texts or charismatic individuals. Postmodern thinkers, especially, have come to appreciate the way what we call "reason" is itself a cultural construction and not the universal and self-evident function of the mind that many philosophers of the past have considered it to be. I always liked the way the 19th century English novelist Elizabeth Gaskell put it. She said: "I'll not listen to reason. Reason always means what someone else has got to say."

Because he views truth as liberating, it's not enough for a belief or an idea to be merely reasonable. According to him, a view or belief must be tested by the results it yields when put into practice. The Buddha would have us ask: Does this belief accord with reality and does it conduce to one's own and others' happiness and freedom? This is what philosophers call the pragmatic criterion of truth. The Buddha further maintained that to guard against the possibility of bias or limitations in one's understanding, acceptable views must be checked against the experience of those who are wise. Of course, these criteria still leave us with other questions: How do we know who is wise? How do we recognize happiness and freedom?

The Buddha addresses these issues in other places. But at this point, I simply want to underscore that a fundamental aspect of Buddhist methodology is the principle of criticism. The Buddha encouraged his followers to subject their beliefs and ideas to rigorous personal testing and not to accept anything—even the Buddha's own teaching—on the mere basis of authority, or antiquity, or rationality. You can imagine what the principle of criticism does when held against the traditions of emerging Hinduism. In effect, the Buddha's teachings implicitly undermined the authority of the Brahmins as well as their sacred Vedic texts. Throughout its history, Hinduism regarded the Buddha's teachings as a major Hindu philosophy but always considered it to be heterodox, or nonorthodox, because Buddhists did not recognize the authority of the Vedas.

In his discourse to his five former disciples, whom he calls *bhikkhus*, the Pali word for monks, the Buddha declares the first of his Noble truths, essentially setting out the primary issue for his worldview.

Now this, *bhikkhus*, is the noble truth of suffering: birth is suffering, aging is suffering, illness is suffering, death is suffering; union with what is displeasing is suffering; separation from what is pleasing is suffering; not to get what one wants is suffering; in brief, the five aggregates subject to clinging are suffering.

Clearly, the key word here is suffering; he mentions it nine times! Later in his life, the Buddha states that he teaches only one thing: suffering and the end of suffering. He was not interested in abstract philosophical questions or dealing with the many speculative matters that had exercised the other teachers of his day. Obviously then, it will be necessary to know what the Buddha means by suffering.

The word that has been translated as "suffering" is the Pali term *dukkha*. Most scholars of Buddhism think that suffering is probably the best English term we have to translate *dukkha*, yet almost all of them agree that it is still an inadequate word. Suffering simply does not effectively convey what the Buddha meant by *dukkha*. Accordingly, you'll find alternative or additional translations, such as pain, illness, unsatisfactoriness, stress, boredom, discontentment, and discomfort. The problem with suffering as the basic translation of *dukkha* is that it's sometimes too strong and too limited to express the Buddha's intent. When I think of suffering, I conjure up images of physical pain and agony, or tremendous grief and other emotional distress. Well, certainly, these things are connoted by the term *dukkha*.

But these images represent only two kinds of *dukkha*. There is the ordinary *dukkha*, the suffering that accompanies injury, sickness, old age, and death. And then there is the *dukkha* of change, the kind of suffering that's caused by loss and being associated with things that one finds unpleasant. The *dukkha* of change means that the Buddha does not deny that there are moments of pleasure, but even such delightful times are subject to *dukkha* because they do not last. Friends and family members die or move away; disagreements break up relationships; money comes and goes; our prized possessions are lost, broken, or decay; happy times always come to an end.

The Buddha, more than any other thinker that I'm aware of, took seriously the impermanent nature of reality and applied it in a thoroughgoing fashion to his Dhamma. Impermanence, or *anicca*, the Pali term, is a salient aspect of the Buddha's vision. He sees the entire world in constant flux, changing from moment to moment, and nothing is exempt from this process. Impermanence is *not* a cause of *dukkha*; but our unwise and unskillful response to the world of change is.

But *dukkha* is not limited to these kinds of experiences. When the Buddha refers to *dukkha* he's describing the fundamental quality of the whole of existence and not merely pointing out that life has moments of tragedy and sorrow. For the Buddha, *dukkha* is insidious and pervasive. Our whole lives, not simply certain occasions, are saturated with the quality of *dukkha*. This is one of the implications of the phrase, "The five aggregates subject to clinging are suffering." As we'll discover in a later talk, the aggregates refer to these constituent elements of human life. The Buddha suggests that the very make-up of human existence is entangled in *dukkha*.

When we think of *dukkha* in these terms, as comprehensive and constant and not simply as episodes in human life, it becomes clear that understanding *dukkha* is not just a problem of translation; it is also an experiential problem as well. We might ask: Why did the Buddha even think it necessary to say that life is suffering? I mean, what kind of insight is that? I want to suggest that what makes *dukkha* a noble truth—and perhaps why the Buddha felt it essential to articulate it—is because we do not fully appreciate the extent to which we suffer or feel the unsatisfactoriness of existence.

The First Noble Truth is not the Buddha's statement of a self-evident fact of life but a challenge for individuals to discover for themselves the depth and breadth of *dukkha* by means of introspection and observation. The Buddha himself hinted at such when he said "This Dhamma that I have attained is profound, hard to see and hard to understand, peaceful and sublime, unattainable by mere reasoning, subtle, to be experienced by the wise." I would even go so far as to say that one cannot realize the nature and extent of *dukkha* until the moment of complete awakening, as the Buddha himself did on the full moon of Vesakha. The true depth of suffering can only be seen from the perspective of the enlightened mind.

These aspects of *dukkha* are some of the reasons that I prefer to use another word, or an additional word, to kind of give us a better sense of what it is. If I had to limit myself to a single word to encapsulate what I think *dukkha* means, it would be the word disappointment. Disappointment is like *dukkha* in the sense that it is a pervasive feature of our lives, though we're not always aware of it. We condition ourselves to ignore many—and maybe most—of our disappointments.

But consider how often during the course of a day we are disappointed, or frustrated. I teach a course at 8 a.m. in the morning, and so I arise at a fairly early hour. (I calculate that I'm getting up just about the time my students are going to bed.) The first thing I experience when the alarm rings is disappointment: sleep is over and the day begins. I get up; I drag myself to the bathroom and look in the mirror—major disappointment. Before I leave the house, I've had other disappointments. The kitchen sink is leaking; I spill coffee on the papers I've been grading; I realize I forgot to pay the utility bill last week. I get to work and a student says something that hurts my ego; the sandwich I had for lunch is not as good as I expected. We pretty much learn to ignore these disappointments, but they soon add up and they begin to affect our mood and our disposition towards others and ourselves.

Besides their insidious and pervasive quality, disappointment and *dukkha* are both the consequences of our own habits of mind. Disappointment is the result of one thing: the failure of reality to conform to our desires and expectations. To call it a failure of reality is a funny way to put it, I suppose, but I think that's the way we often experience it. Reality, of course, is not to blame. Reality just is what it is; the problem is with our desires and expectations. So it would be more accurate to say that our desires and expectations do not conform to reality, and when they don't we are liable to suffer. When the Buddha characterizes *dukkha* as not getting what you want and getting what you don't want, he is implicitly putting the onus on us, not on the thing that we want or don't want.

Elsewhere he mentions another element that contributes to *dukkha*. No doubt, not getting what you want causes disappointment, but so does getting what you want. Both the frustration of desire and the fulfillment of desire contribute to human suffering. In our society in which the way to happiness is virtually defined as the fulfillment of wishes, such a claim must sound odd. But for the Buddha, the problem with achieving our desires is that it really doesn't satisfy us in the way we had hoped, and we end up desiring more and more to try to attain the kind of satisfaction that we so badly want. The Buddha said:

> Were there a mountain all made of gold,
> doubled that would not be enough
> to satisfy a single man.

Ever since my college days, I wanted nothing so badly as to have the title "Doctor" attached to my name. I'm not even sure from where that desire came from. But I craved it like nothing else. When the day finally came that I received my Ph.D., amid all the fanfare and festivities, I couldn't help but notice a gnawing sensation of discontentment. For several months afterwards, I felt increasingly depressed. It took me a while, but I realized that I had expected that somehow receiving this degree would radically transform my life; that my self-confidence would soar and I would command great respect and admiration of others; that I would be capable of superior intellectual feats. The disappointment came because none of that happened. There was no radical transformation as I expected. I felt some satisfaction in attaining my long-held ambition, but that satisfaction didn't last long. It was soon forgotten in a plethora of new goals and new expectations.

Desires, whether they are fulfilled or frustrated, only beget more desires. Trying to fulfill desires is looking for happiness in all the wrong places. The reason we look in all the wrong places is that we really don't know what it will take to satisfy us. I'll never forget the experience of watching a little boy of about three, bitterly crying and frantically running down the aisles of a department store, screaming, "I need something! I need something!" When his parents finally caught up with him, they could get no more out him than that he needed something but he had no idea what it was. Something about that boy's earnest plea sounded so authentically human to me; I knew just how he felt. We all think we need something, but we're at a loss for saying what it is.

By comparing *dukkha* to disappointment, I have emphasized the role of desire in creating unhappiness. This is also the connection the Buddha makes. But his analysis does not stop here. Desire itself has antecedents, basic causes that urge us to want and crave for things. In the Second Noble Truth, the Buddha explains the factors that led us to desire in the first place. Thus the Buddha's second truth concerns the cause of suffering. In our next talk, we'll examine his view on the deeper sources of *dukkha.* Once we've considered those sources, we'll be prepared for the third truth, the end of suffering.

Timeline

B.C.E.

c. 3000–1500 .... Indus Valley culture (South Asia)

c. 2300–1200 .... Composition of the Rig Veda (Central and South Asia)

c. 1500–1000 .... Migration of Aryans into the Indus Valley (South Asia)

c. 1500–1045 .... Shang Dynasty (East Asia)

c. 1045–221 .... Zhou Dynasty (East Asia)

c. 1045–771 .... Western Zhou Dynasty (East Asia)

c. 1000 .... Migration of Aryans into Gangetic plains (South Asia)

c. 1200 .... Zoroaster (West Asia)

c. 1000? .... Composition of the Gathas of the Avesta (West Asia)

c. 800–200 .... Composition of the Upanishads (South Asia)

771–221 .... Eastern Zhou (East Asia)

722–481 .... Spring and Autumn Period (East Asia)

595–573 .... Ministry of Ezekiel (West Asia)

586–536 .... Babylonian Captivity of Judah (West Asia)

582–507 .... Pythagoras of Samos (Greece)

c. 551–479 .... Confucius (East Asia)

c. 540–468 .... Vardhamana Mahavira (South Asia) (tradition says he was born in 599)

535–475 .... Heraclitus of Ephesus (Greece)

c. 490–410 .... Siddhattha Gotama, the Buddha (South Asia) (tradition says he was born in 563)

475 or 403–221 ....Period of the Warring States (East Asia)

c. 470–390..................................Mozi (East Asia)

470–399 ....Socrates of Athens (Greece)

c. 427–347..................................Plato (Greece)

c. 385–c. 312..............................Mencius (East Asia)

c. 384–322..................................Aristotle (Greece)

369–286 ....Zhuangzi (East Asia)

327–325 ....Campaign of Alexander the Great in India

c. 310–c. 219..............................Xunzi (East Asia)

273–232 ....Reign of Ashoka (South Asia)

c. 250..Composition of the Book of Qoheleth (Ecclesiastes)

221–206 ....Qin Dynasty (East Asia)

206 B.C.E.–220 C.E...................Han Dynasty (East Asia)

c. 200 B.C.E.–100 C.E..............Composition of the Bhagavad-Gita (South Asia)

c. 200–100..................................First Buddha images in Gandhāra (South Asia)

c. 167–164..................................Final redaction of the Book of Daniel

c. 150..Pali Canon put in writing (South Asia)

c. 100 B.C.E.–100 C.E..............Rise of Mahayana Buddhism (South Asia)

c. 4 B.C.E.–29 C.E....................Jesus of Nazareth (West Asia)

C.E.

c. 50..Introduction of Buddhism to China (East Asia)

570–632 ....Muhammad (West Asia)

c. 788–820 .... Sankara (South Asia)

c. 1077–1157 .... Ramanuja (South Asia)

1469-1539 .... Guru Nanak Dev

1844–1900 .... Friedrich Nietzsche

1869–1948 .... Mohandas K. Gandhi

1883–1969 .... Karl Jaspers

Glossary

Scholars often use diacritical marks in transliterating some of the languages used in this course. Because one may occasionally encounter the diacritics, alternative spellings are given in parentheses to help avoid confusion. The Chinese terms have been transliterated according to the Pinyin system rather than the older Wade-Giles.

Agam Sutras (Āgam Sutras): The central Jain scriptures, believed by Jains to be the words of Vardhamana Mahavira as recalled by his chief disciple, Indrabhuti.

ahimsa **(*ahimsā*)**: The practice of doing no harm to living beings, according to Hinduism, Buddhism, and Jainism.

Ahriman: The evil god in Zoroastrian theology; also known as Aeshma and Angra Mainyu.

ahuras: The Avestan word for the gods or spirits aligned with the principle of good.

airyana vaejah **(*airyana waējah*)**: "The land of the noble" in the ancient Iranian language; the name from which *Iran* is derived.

Analects: The collection of sayings and dialogues of Confucius, compiled (and at least partially composed) by his students after his death; known in Chinese as the *Lunyu* ("Conversations"). This text is the basis for what we know about Confucius's life and teachings.

Ananda: The Buddha's personal attendant, who memorized the Buddha's discourses and recited them at the First Buddhist Council; his recollections became the Suttas of the Pali Canon.

anatta: The Pali term for Buddha's denial of a permanent, substantial self or soul. Translated as "no-self" or "not-self"; known in Sanskrit as *anatman*, or "no-*atman*."

ancestor reverence: Treating one's forebears as living spirits whom one should honor, worship, and consult on important family decisions; an especially important practice throughout Chinese religious history.

anekanta **(*anekānta*)**: "Many-sided"; the Jain idea that the world is composed of an infinite number of material and spiritual substances, each with an infinite number of qualities and manifestations. Because of this complexity of the universe, all claims to truth must be tentative.

anicca: Pali word for impermanence.

arahant: A living individual who has attained awakening in Buddhism.

Ardhanari (Ardhanārī): Iconic representation of the god as half Shiva, half Parvati; intended to symbolize the male/female, form/power aspects of the divine.

ariya: Noble.

Arjuna: The warrior whose ethical dilemma forms the basis of a wide-ranging dialogue with Lord Krishna in the Bhagavad-Gita.

Aryans (Āryans): The central Asian pastoral nomads who migrated into Iran and India prior to the Axial Age.

Aryavarta (Āryavarta): "The land of the noble"; the Indo-Aryan name for their homeland in northern India.

ascetic: One who practices forms of self-denial (for example, fasting, celibacy, abstinence from luxury and comforts) in order to attain higher spiritual goals.

asha: The Iranian principle of right and order; opposed to *druj*, the principle of disorder and chaos.

ashavans: Those who follow and revere *asha*.

Ashoka (Aśoka), King: Ruler of the Mauryan Empire in India (r. 273–232 B.C.E.); a Buddhist convert who was responsible for the spread of Buddhism throughout India and other parts of Asia.

asuras: Sanskrit term for a class of divinities opposed to the *devas*; usually demonic in character.

***atman* (*ātman*)**: The soul. Initially understood as the breath in the early Vedic era, the *atman* is later regarded by Hindus as immortal and transmigratory.

Avesta: The central scripture of Zoroastrianism. The most sacred sections of the Avesta are the Gathas, or Hymns of Zoroaster.

Avestan: The Indo-European language in which the Zoroastrian Avesta was originally written.

avijja **(*avijjā*)**: Pali word for ignorance or misknowing.

awakening: Traditional metaphor for the experience of realizing the highest spiritual wisdom. When Siddhattha Gotama completely understood the causal factors of *dukkha* and the way to *nibbana* while sitting under the Bodhi tree, he claimed to have had this experience; sometimes called enlightenment.

Axial Age: Term coined by philosopher Karl Jaspers to denote the era of exceptional religious and philosophical creativity between 800–200 B.C.E. that gave rise to the major world religions.

Babylonian Captivity: The deportation and exile of a large segment of the population of Judah to Babylon by King Nebuchadrezzar (586–536 B.C.E.); this event marks the start of the Jewish Diaspora; also known as the Exile.

Banaras (Banāras): The holiest city in India; situated on the Ganges River in the contemporary state of Uttar Pradesh. The Buddha gave his first discourse at the Deer Park near Banaras; also known as Varanasi and Kashi.

bao: Chinese word for the desire to repay kindness with a similar act of kindness.

Bhagavad-Gita (Bhagavad-Gītā): Much-beloved Hindu text recounting the dialogue of Lord Krishna and Arjuna before the war between the Kurus and the Pandavas.

bhikkhu/bhikkhuni: Buddhist monk/nun.

Bodhi tree: Buddhist term for the tree under which Siddhattha Gotama realized awakening and became the Buddha.

Brahman: The Absolute, ultimate reality. Originally, Brahman was the Vedic word for the power inherent in ritual; later, the term came to designate the highest reality beyond all conceptualization.

Brahmin (Brāhmin): The caste of priests and intellectuals.

Buddha: One who grasps the causes of suffering and puts an end to it. In the Theravada Buddhist tradition, *the Buddha* is a title reserved for one who realizes awakening on his or her own; those who see *nibbana* through the teaching of a Buddha are called *arahants*. *Buddha* literally means the "Awakened One."

Buddhism: Religious tradition whose origins date to the ferment that initiated Jainism and classical Hinduism. Following the conversion of Emperor Ashoka, Buddhism became the dominant religion of India and remained so until the advent of Islam returned Hinduism to the ascendancy.

caste: Portuguese term to describe the stratification of Hindu society based on occupation and purity. Caste usually refers to the *varna* system, the fourfold classification of Brahmins, Kshatriyas, Vaishyas, and Shudras.

Celestial Masters: Early movement of the Daoist "church" whose followers sought to attain immortality through elixirs.

Charlie Chan: Character in American movies in the 1930s and 1940s who shaped popular Western impressions of Confucius.

cosmic maintenance: The pre-Axial function of religion in which the processes of the world are supported or controlled by human activity.

cosmogony: Creation story.

***daeva* (*daēva*)**: Avestan cognate of *deva*, a "shiny one"; considered by Zoroaster to be a class of malevolent divinities. This is the word from which *devil* derives.

Dao: The reality underlying and governing the universe; Chinese for "the way."

Daodejing: The Chinese classic (*jing*) of the way (*dao*) and the power (*de*); the basis of philosophical Daoism.

daojia: Philosophical Daoism; literally, the School of the Way.

daojiao: The Daoist "church."; literally, the Teaching of the Way.

***darshana* (*darśana*)**: To "take *darshana*" means to see and to be seen by the deity. *Darshana* is also the word for a philosophical system, such as Yoga or Vedanta.

Day of Judgment: The end of the world as we know it. According to Zoroaster, the Day of Judgment will entail the final triumph of good over evil; this concept also appears in Judaism, Christianity, and Islam.

de: Virtue or power.

Deer Park: The site of the Buddha's first discourse; located in present-day Sarnath, near Banaras, India.

deva: Sanskrit term for god; literally, "shiny one."

devi (***devī***): Sanskrit term for goddess.

Dhamma: The teaching of the Buddha.

dharma: Sacred duty according to caste; the principle of cosmic order; "religion." *Dharma* is the principle that succeeded the Vedic concept of *rta*.

di: Chinese term for Earth.

Di: Shortened form of Shangdi, the early Chinese high god.

Digambaras: One of the two orders of monastics in Jainism; members of this order renounce even their clothes, inspiring their name, the "sky-clad."

divination: The practice of communicating with the spirits through the interpretation of tangible elements.

dragon bones: Nickname for the inscribed cattle bones used for divination in the Shang Dynasty; so-called by modern Chinese pharmacies when the bones were sold as ingredients in medicines.

druj: Avestan term for the principle of disorder, evil, chaos; Sanskrit: *druh*.

drujvants: "Followers of the Lie"; those who, according to Zoroaster, aligned themselves with the principle of *druj*.

dukkha: Pali term usually translated as suffering, disappointment, and unsatisfactoriness.

Durga (Durgā): One of the manifestations of the goddess in Hinduism.

Dyaoš, Dyaus-Pitr: Ancient names for the high god in the Avesta and Vedas, respectively; cognates of Zeus and Jupiter.

Eastern Zhou: See **Zhou Dynasty**.

epistemology: The philosophical study of knowledge.

equanimity: The attitude of calmness and serenity.

eschaton: The end of time.

ethicization: The interpretation of events or practices in ethical terms; one of the characteristic processes of Axial Age religions.

evil, problem of: The dilemma posed by the belief in a god who is considered both all-good and all-powerful in a world in which evil exists; logically, according to the traditional formulation of the problem, if evil exists, then god must be either not all good or not all powerful.

Ezekiel: Prophet of ancient Judah.

ficus religiosa: Scientific name for the Bodhi tree.

filial piety: The practice of reverencing and honoring one's parents; Chinese: *xiao*.

Five Aggregates of Being: According to the Buddha's teaching, these are the ever-changing forces comprising what is conventionally called the self: matter, sensation, perception, mental formations, and consciousness.

Five Precepts: The vows taken by Buddhists to guide wholesome action. They include the promise to abstain from harming sentient beings, to abstain from false speech, to abstain from misusing sexuality, to abstain from taking what is not offered, and to abstain from taking intoxicating substances.

Four Noble Truths: The essence of the Buddha's teaching as expressed in his first discourse following awakening. The truths are *dukkha* (suffering and disappointment), the cause of *dukkha*, the cessation of *dukkha*, and the Eightfold Path to *nibbana*.

Four Sights: The experience that prompted Siddhattha Gotama to renounce home life to seek an end to suffering. According to tradition, Gotama saw a sick person, an old person, a corpse, and a *samana* in an excursion outside the palace precincts.

Frashokereti: The "making glorious"; Zoroaster's term for the eschatological battle in which the forces of good defeat the forces of evil once and for all, ushering in an everlasting reign of peace and harmony.

Gandhara (Gandhāra): The region of northwestern India and eastern Afghanistan where the first anthropomorphic Buddha images were produced some 500 years after the life of the Buddha.

Gathas (Gāthās): The "verses"; part of the oldest Avesta, the foundational scripture of Zoroaster's religion. These verses are believed to have been actually composed by Zoroaster himself under moments of religious inspiration.

Gaya (Bodh Gaya): Northeastern India town, location of the Buddha's awakening.

ghosts: In Chinese religion, the spirits of the unburied.

Gotama, Siddhattha: Given name of the Shakyan (Śākyan) noble who became the Buddha.

guru: Teacher.

Han Dynasty: The family who ruled China from 206 B.C.E.–220 C.E., one of the most prosperous and stable periods in Chinese history.

Haoma: See **Soma**.

heptad: "The seven"; the spirits or gods, including Ahura Mazda, seen by Zoroaster in his call to be a prophet.

High Hara: The holiest mountain on Earth, where souls would be judged on the fourth day following death, according to Zoroastrian theology.

Hinduism: The Western term for the Indian religions that regard the Vedas as the highest authority.

householder: The second stage of life for both men and women of caste. At the householder stage, Hindus marry, raise children, work, and contribute to the good of family and society.

idolatry: Confusing the ultimate reality with what is less than ultimate.

Indo-Aryans (Indo-Āryans): Modern designation for the Central Asian people who eventually settled in India in the second millennium B.C.E.

Indo-European: Modern term for the Central Asian ancestors of many of the inhabitants of India and Europe.

Indo-Iranians: Modern term for the Central Asian people who migrated southward from the steppes and eventually split, with some going to Iran (the Iranians or Irano-Aryans) and some to India (the Indo-Aryans).

Indra: The war god of the Aryans; the ascendant deity of the Rig Veda; the *deva* who also controlled the waters.

Indus Valley culture: One of the great cultures of the ancient world; flourished from c. 3000–c. 1500 B.C.E. in northwestern India along the Indus River system; also known as the Harappan (Harappān) civilization.

"Inner Chapters": Part of the Zhuangzi, a text of early philosophical Daoism; possibly written by Zhuangzi himself.

ista-devata **(*ista-devatā*)**: One's personal deity of choice in Hinduism.

Jainism: Religious tradition whose origins date to the ferment that initiated Buddhism and classical Hinduism. Jainism and Buddhism are regarded by Hindus as heterodox philosophies because they deny Vedic authority.

Jambudvipa (Jambudvīpa): "The island of the rose-apple tree"; a term for the earthly realm used by Jains, Buddhists, and Hindus.

Jaspers, Karl: German philosopher (1883–1969); often associated with Existentialism; coined the term *die Achsenzeit*, or Axial Age, to designate the period from 800–200 B.C.E.

jina: A spiritual victor in Jainism.

jivanmukta: In Hinduism, a living, liberated soul.

jnana **(*jñāna*)**: Sanskrit word for knowledge; related to the Greek *gnosis*.

jnana-marga: The path of liberation from *samsara* based on the quest for wisdom and the dissolution of illusion. The *jnana-marga* usually requires ascetic practice and great discipline.

junzi: The gentleman or noble man in Confucianism; the most important ideal type for Confucius.

karma: Action and its consequences. In the Hindu view, karma is a principle of justice, ensuring that the effects of one's actions return to the agent. Karma is what binds the soul to the cycle of endless existence and determines its station in future existences.

Kisagotami: A young woman who begs the Buddha to bring her dead son back to life; the Buddha instructs her to find a mustard seed from a home that has never been touched by death.

Krishna: One of the principal avatars or manifestations of the Hindu god Vishnu; Krishna instructs Arjuna on devotion to god in the Bhagavad-Gita.

Kshatriyas (Kśatriyas): The caste of warriors and administrators.

Kushinagara: Northeastern Indian village near the site of the Buddha's *parinibbana*, or final liberation.

Laozi: The legendary founder of Daoism and the traditional author of the Daodejing, which is also known as the Laozi.

Legalism: The Chinese philosophical school opposed to Confucianism. Embraced by the Qin Dynasty, Legalism advocated a strict law-and-order approach to maintaining social stability.

li: Originally, the Chinese term for religious rituals and ceremonies. Confucius broadened the term to include everyday behavior and manners.

lingam: Representation of the phallus. Thousands of stone lingams were discovered in the excavations of the Indus Valley civilization and are presumed to be associated with rites of fertility. Today, the lingam and yoni (its vulvic counterpart) symbolize the god Shiva and his Shakti.

Magi: Term for the "wise men from the East" who visited Jesus as an infant; derived from *magus*, an Old Iranian word for priest.

Mahavira (Mahāvīra): The "Great Hero"; a traditional title for Vardhamana (Vardhamāna), the 24th Tirthankara of Jainism.

Mahayana (Mahāyāna): Sanskrit for the "Great Vehicle"; a branch of Buddhism that developed in the early centuries of the Common Era that brought a new understanding of the Buddha and the nature of liberation.

manas: Vedic word for that which animates the body; translates as mind, heart, or life force.

Mandate of Heaven: The moral authority by which the ruler rules. The concept—believed to have been first articulated by the Dan, the

Duke of Zhou—was used to justify the Zhou overthrow of the Shang Dynasty; Chinese: *Tianming*.

mantra: A sound or phrase embodying sacred power.

Mara: The tempter in Buddhism; as Siddhattha Gotama approached awakening while sitting under the Bodhi tree, Mara attempted to thwart attainment of his goal.

maya **(*māyā*)**: Illusion; the veil over reality that prevents the unenlightened from seeing the world as it truly is. *Maya* causes us to see multiplicity where there is in reality only unity.

Maya, Queen: Wife of King Suddhodhana and mother of Siddhattha Gotama. Queen Maya died seven days after the birth of Siddhattha, who was then raised by Queen Prajapati, Maya's sister.

Mazda: An *ahura* of early Iranian religion; according to Zoroaster, Mazda was the principal (and perhaps sole) benevolent deity, locked in combat with the Evil One until the end of time.

Middle Way: The course of life promoted by the Buddha, in which one avoids the extremes of indulgence and deprivation.

Mithra: One of the major gods of Indo-Iranian religion; initially associated with promise-keeping.

Mohism: School of Chinese philosophy developed by Mozi. In contrast to Confucianism, Mohism advocated universal love of humanity.

moksha **(*mokśa*)**: Release or liberation from the wheel of *samsara*. Pursued and conceptualized in a variety of ways, *moksha* is the ultimate goal of Hindus.

Mozi: Chinese philosopher who advocated "impartial caring" or "universal love" and criticized Confucius's belief that one should love others in proportion to the benefit one receives from them.

Nachiketas: Young Brahmin in the Upanishads who engaged Yama, the King of the Underworld, in a dialogue about death.

Nanak Dev, Guru: The founder of Sikhism (1469–1539).

nibbana **(*nibbāna*)**: Pali term for the end of suffering and rebirth; Sanskrit: *nirvāna*.

Nietzsche, Friedrich: German philosopher (1844–1900); author of *Also Sprach Zarathustra*.

Nirguna Brahman: Ultimate reality without qualities. This term is used to describe the aspect of Brahman that is ineffable.

Noble Eightfold Path: The Buddha's prescription for realizing *nibbana*; includes right understanding, right intentions, right speech, right action, right livelihood, right effort, right concentration, and right mindfulness.

Noruz: "New Day"; the celebration of the new year in Iranian religion.

no-self, not-self: The Buddha's denial of a permanent, substantial self or soul; Pali: *anatta*, Sanskrit: *anatman*.

Odes, Book of: A collection of more than 300 poems from the early Zhou Dynasty to the Spring and Autumn periods. Perhaps the earliest such collection in Chinese literature; considered part of the *Wu Jing*, the Five Classics of Confucianism; Chinese: *Shi Jing*.

One Hundred Philosophers, Period of: The Chinese era during the late Spring and Autumn and Warring States periods in which many schools of philosophy were established, including Confucianism and Daoism.

oracle: A communication from the spirit world or the medium of that communication.

pairi-daeza: Ancient Iranian term meaning "enclosed garden"; the basis for the word *paradise*.

Pali (Pāli): A simplified vernacular form of Sanskrit in which the discourses of the Buddha were first written.

Pali Canon: The earliest collection of Buddhist scriptures, comprising the Suttas (discourses), the Vinaya (monastic rules), and Abhidhamma (the codification of the Dhamma).

***parinibbana* (*parinibbāna*)**: The final liberation of a fully realized person.

Parsis: The Zoroastrians (and their descendants) who fled to India to escape the Islamic conquest of Iran.

Prajapati, Queen: Aunt and foster-mother to Siddhattha Gotama; sister of Queen Maya; the first Buddhist nun.

prophet: One who speaks for the god, often urging people back to an authentic form of religious practice at a time when religion has become corrupt.

***puja* (*pūjā*)**: Sanskrit word for the ritual worship of a god, goddess, or object representing sacred reality.

Purusha: The primordial human who was sacrificed and dismembered to create the parts of the cosmos, society, and the ritual according to the Rig Veda.

Qin Dynasty: The period of Chinese history between the Zhou and Han Dynasties (221–206 B.C.E.); during the Qin, China was unified and Legalism was the dominant philosophy.

Rahula (Rāhula): Son of Siddhattha Gotama and his wife, Yashodhara; in later life, Rahula became a Buddhist monk.

Ramanuja (Rāmānuja): Indian philosopher (c. 1077–1157 C.E.); founded the school of the Vishishtadvaita Vedanta, or qualified non-dualism.

redeath: The Vedic belief that the soul may ascend to heaven at death, live there for a while until it exhausts its karma, and die again to be reborn on Earth.

ren: Chinese word for humaneness.

renunciation: In the South Asian context, renunciation is giving up home, possessions, social standing, and family ties to "go forth" into the world to seek liberation from *samsara*.

Rig Veda: The oldest and most important of the Vedas; compiled between 2300 and 1200 B.C.E. The Rig Veda comprises more than 1,000 hymns to various Vedic deities; *rig* means "praise."

ritual purity: The state of cleanliness that is necessary for being in the presence of the sacred.

rose-apple tree: A south and southeast Asian tree with small edible fruits. It was under this variety of tree that Siddhattha had his first meditation experience as a boy.

rta: The Vedic principle of order and harmony.

Saguna Brahman: That aspect of Brahman that can be conceptualized and discussed.

samana: Pali term for a wandering ascetic. Sanskrit: *shramana*.

***samsara* (*samsāra*)**: The phenomenal world of change and transience. *Samsara* denotes the situation in which the soul sequentially incarnates in different bodies at different levels of existence.

Sangha: The order of monks and nuns in Buddhism.

Sanskrit: Indo-European language in which the Vedas were composed.

saoshyant: A savior or judge who appears at the end of time, according to Zoroaster; literally, "one who brings benefit."

satya: Sanskrit word for truth, specifically, the *higher* truth.

***satyagraha* (*satyāgraha*)**: Literally, "grasping for the truth"; Gandhi's term for his philosophy and practice of non-violent resistance to injustice.

Shakya (Śākya): The clan of Siddhattha Gotama.

Shang Di: Term for the high god of early Chinese religion; also known as Di.

Shang Dynasty: Circa 1500–1045 B.C.E.; the earliest Chinese dynasty for which there is historical evidence.

Shankara (Śankara): Indian philosopher (c. 788–820 C.E.); founder of the school of Advaita Vedanta, or non-dualism, based on the Upanishads.

Shiva (Śiva): One the great cosmic gods of Hinduism and the center of one of Hinduism's largest and most important religions.

***shrauta* (*śrauta*) ritual**: Ordinarily complex Vedic ceremonies using the verses of the Vedas for the purpose of maintaining divine-human relations.

***shruti* (*śruti*)**: Sacred literature of the highest authority in Hinduism; believed to have been revealed to the ancient *rishis*, *shruti* includes the Rig Veda and the Upanishads.

shu: Chinese word for reciprocity.

Shudras (Śudras): The lowest of the four *varnas* in India; the caste of peasants and servants.

Siddhartha (Siddhārtha), King: The father of Vardhamana Mahavira, the 24th Tirthankara of Jainism.

Siddhattha: The given name of the one who became the Buddha; *Siddhattha* means "he who attains the goal."

Sikhism: An indigenous Indian religion inspired by Kabir, a mystic-poet from Varanasi, and founded by Guru Nanak, a Hindu from Punjab. Both men condemned Hindu and Muslim sectarianism and sought to establish authentic worship of the one true god.

Soma: The Sanskrit name for the god whose manifestation as a particular plant produced visions and a sense of well-being in those who ingested it. Avestan: Haoma.

Son of Man: Jewish concept of the individual who appears at the apocalypse as a divine judge; the title Jesus most often applies to himself in the Gospel of Mark.

Soul of the Bull: The divine being in ancient Iranian religion who sustained and nurtured animal life.

Spring and Autumn Period: The first of two eras of the Eastern Zhou Dynasty in China; circa 722–481 B.C.E.

***stupa* (*stūpa*)**: A Buddhist reliquary; also known as *dagoba* and *pagoda*.

Suddhodhana, King: Ruler of the Shakya kingdom; husband of Queen Maya and Queen Prajapati; father of Siddhattha Gotama.

Suttas: The discourses of Buddha.

Shvetambaras (Śvetāmbaras): One of the two orders of monastics in Jainism; the "white-robed."

swastika: Ancient Indo-Aryan symbol for the Sun.

sympathetic magic: The practice of attempting to affect realities by manipulating objects or words representing those realities.

Taijitu: The Chinese diagram representing the relationship of the yin and yang principles.

tanha: Pali term for craving; literally, "thirst."

Theravada (Theravāda): The "way of the elders"; the oldest extant variety of Buddhism. Also called *Southern Buddhism* because of its prominence in South and Southeast Asia.

Three Sages, Era of the: Mythic period of early Chinese history.

Three Sovereigns, Era of the: Mythic period of early Chinese history.

tian: Chinese word for heaven.

Tianming: See **Mandate of Heaven**.

Tirthankara: According to Jainism, one who teaches the truth and the way to liberation; literally, a bridge-builder or ford-maker.

transcendental consciousness: Term used by S. N. Eisenstadt to refer to the Axial Age thrust to gain a larger or deeper understanding of the nature of reality.

transmigration of the soul: Reincarnation; *samsara*.

Triple Practice: The traditional division of the Noble Eightfold Path into Moral Behavior, Concentration, and Wisdom.

Triple Refuge: A statement of Buddhist identity: "I take refuge in the Buddha; I take refuge in the Dhamma; and I take refuge in the Sangha."

Trishala (Triśala), Queen: Wife of King Siddhartha and mother of Vardhamana Mahavira, the 24th Tirthankara of Jainism.

Upanishads (Upaniśads): Collection of early Hindu writings in which the ideas of transmigration of the soul and the identity of Brahman and *atman* are first proposed; considered *shruti*, the highest form of authority in Hinduism.

Vaishyas (Vaiśyas): The caste of farmers, cattle herders, artisans, and businesspeople.

Vajrayana (Vajrayāna): The third major form of Buddhism, practiced mainly in Tibet and Mongolia; literally, the "diamond" or "thunderbolt" vehicle.

Varuna: Indo-Iranian god associated with promise-keeping.

Vedanta (Vedānta): The "end of the Vedas." Vedanta is one of the most important and influential of the Hindu philosophies. Deriving inspiration particularly from the Upanishads, the last part of the Vedas, Vedanta emphasizes unity of the soul and the Absolute.

Vedas: Sacred wisdom believed to have been revealed to ancient *rishis*. The Vedas are now the most sacred of Hindu scriptures.

Vesak: Festival that celebrates the birth, awakening, and *parinibbana* of the Buddha.

via negativa: The way of negation; a theological technique of referring to ultimate reality by saying what it is not.

Vishnu: A minor Vedic god who ultimately became one of Hinduism's most important gods and the object of a major Hindu religion; according to tradition, Vishnu has assumed 10 principal manifestations, including Krishna, Rama, and the Buddha.

Warring States, Period of: The second of the two eras of the Eastern Zhou Dynasty in China, from 475 or 403 B.C.E. until 221 B.C.E.; a time in which the warlords of small feudal kingdoms sought to annex other states to extend and consolidate their power.

Wen, King: The symbolic first ruler of the Zhou Dynasty.

Western Zhou: See **Zhou Dynasty**.

Wu: The man who led the overthrow of Shang rulers and established the Zhou Dynasty of China; son of King Wen.

Wu Jing: The "Five Classics"; used by Confucianism as a basis for study; includes the Book of Odes (*Shī Jīng*), the Book of Changes (*Yì Jīng*), the Book of Rites (*Lǐ Jīng*), the Book of History (*Shū Jīng*), and the Spring and Autumn Annals (*Lín Jīng*).

wu wei: Actionless action; one of the fundamental virtues of Daoism.

yajña: Sacrifice; Avestan: *yasna*.

Yama: The Vedic/Hindu god of death and ruler of the underworld; Avestan: Yima.

Yashodhara (Yaśodhara): Wife of Siddhattha Gotama; mother of Rahula; later a Buddhist nun.

yazatas: Class of divinities in Zoroastrianism associated with the principle of good; perhaps the prototype for angels in the religions of Semitic origin.

yin/yang: The Chinese principles accounting for change; yin is associated with the feminine and yang with the masculine; the Chinese ideal is to maintain a balance between yin and yang.

yoga: A discipline for the purposes of enlightenment and liberation. *Yoga* literally means "yoke." In a narrower sense, *Yoga* refers to a specific school of orthodox philosophy given classical expression in the Yoga Sutras of Patañjali.

Zhou, Duke of (Dan): The brother of King Wu and founder of the Zhou Dynasty, who ruled as regent for his nephew following Wu's death; the Duke of Zhou embodied many of the highest virtues, according to Confucius.

Zhou Dynasty: The period of Chinese history between the Shang and the Qin Dynasties (1045–221 B.C.E.); divided into the Western and Eastern Zhou when invaders forced the move of the capital eastward.

Zoroastrianism: The religion based on Zoroaster's reforms of ancient Iranian religion.

Biographical Notes

Confucius (c. 551–479 B.C.E.): Perhaps the most influential Chinese philosopher. Known as Kongzi, or Master Kong, he was born in the state of Lu, the son of a relatively poor family of the lower nobility. Although he aspired to serve as a political advisor to a duke or king, the most important post he held was the equivalent of a police commissioner in his home province. Confucius gathered disciples and taught throughout his later life and occasionally consulted with various kings and government officials. He maintained that human harmony lies in moral action and good government, which support the well-being of the state and the people. In the Han Dynasty, Confucianism was adopted as the state ideology, and Confucius himself was later deified and worshiped.

Gotama, Siddhattha, the Buddha (c. 490–410 B.C.E.): A nobleman in northeastern India who became a *samana* at age 29 when he was faced with the realities of sickness, old age, and death. After 6 years of zealous ascetic practices, he decided to pursue what he called the Middle Way. While engaged in meditation under a tree, he attained complete understanding of the dynamics of suffering and anguish and how to eradicate them. For the next 45 years, the Buddha traveled throughout the Gangetic plains of India, teaching his Dhamma and establishing a community of followers. At his death, the unburned remains of his body were housed in reliquaries at various locations significant in his life. (Tradition says he was born in 563 B.C.E.)

Laozi: Probably a fictitious character invented by the early Daoist philosophers to provide a counterpart to Confucius. Daoist tradition holds that Laozi was an older contemporary of Confucius and that the two were acquainted. One legend even suggests that Confucius was one of Laozi's students. Daoist stories relate several encounters between Laozi and Confucius, and the former is depicted as gaining the upper hand in philosophical debate. He is reputed to have written the Daodejing, or the Laozi, as it is sometimes called, when asked to leave a record of his wisdom by the city gatekeeper as he departed social life to spend his old age in solitude. In later Daoism, Laozi is deified and worshiped.

Mahavira, Vardhamana (c. 599–527 or 540–468 B.C.E.): The 24th Tirthankara of Jainism. Born to King Siddhartha and Queen Trishala of the kingdom of Vaishali in northeastern India, Vardhamana became a *samana* at age 30, following the deaths of his parents. After 12 years of ascetic practice, he attained the state of omniscience and was recognized as a Tirthankara, one who shows the way to liberation from *samsara*. His efforts also earned him the title *the Mahavira*, or the "Great Hero," the epithet by which he is best known. From his enlightenment until his death, he taught in northeastern India and amassed a large community of monastic and lay followers.

Mencius (c. 385–c. 312 B.C.E.): Chinese philosopher who was one of the first and most influential interpreters of Confucius. Mencius, or Mengzi, as he was known, was a student of Confucius's grandson and later adopted the peripatetic ways of the sage and consulted with the rulers of various Chinese principalities. He was especially interested in the question of human nature and argued that human beings were fundamentally good. The evil that humans do comes from social conditioning, not from our basic natures, he believed. His teachings were compiled by his students into the Mencius.

Xunzi (c. 310–c. 219 B.C.E.): An early Confucian thinker who opposed Mencius's position on human nature. A native of the state of Zhao in north-central China, Xunzi provided a rigorous explanation and defense of Confucian thought in the work that bears his name, the Xunzi. Unlike Mencius, Xunzi believed that human nature was not fundamentally good, and hence, human beings required thoughtful and deliberate education to become good people. Along with Confucius and Mencius, Xunzi was one of the architects of Chinese Confucianism.

Zhuangzi (c. 369–286 B.C.E.): The Daoist thinker who was most responsible for drawing out the mystical implications of the foundational Daoist principles. Unlike other philosophers of the Warring States Period, Zhuangzi was decidedly disinterested in political and social affairs. His philosophy reflects the interests of the solitary person in communion with the ultimate reality. Zhuangzi's thought revels in the excitement of change and surrenders to its inevitability. The "Inner Chapters" of the text called the Zhuangzi, which are believed to come from Zhuangzi himself, are a collection of compelling stories, parables, and anecdotes that are intended more to question conventional wisdom and practices than to establish a systematic philosophical position.

Zoroaster: Greek transliteration of the name *Zarathustra*, an Iranian prophet and founder of the religion of Zoroastrianism, or Mazdaism. There is no consensus on when Zoroaster lived. Some scholarly estimates suggest that he lived as early as the 15th century B.C.E. and as late as the 6th century B.C.E. Zoroaster was a priest who felt called to urge his contemporaries to worship the Ahura Mazda exclusively. According to Zoroaster, Mazda was the one true god of goodness who was in conflict with the god of evil and his minions. In order to attain salvation, individuals must align themselves with Mazda against the forces of evil. Zoroaster's thought may have influenced many of the important beliefs of later Judaism, Christianity, and Islam.

Bibliography

Essential Reading:

Adler, Joseph A. *Chinese Religious Traditions.* Upper Saddle River, NJ: Prentice Hall, 2002. This is one of the best short introductions to the history of Chinese religions that I've seen. It is accessible to the lay reader and scholarly in its research. Charts and photographs nicely augment the exposition.

Boyce, Mary. *Zoroastrians: Their Religious Beliefs and Practices.* London and New York: Routledge, 2001. Mary Boyce was a professor of Iranian Studies and perhaps the world's leading scholar of Zoroastrianism up until her death in 2006. *Zoroastrians: Their Religious Beliefs and Practices* was her effort to provide a comprehensive history of the religion, from the earliest times to the present, in a single volume accessible to the intelligent layperson. It is probably the best text in English for gaining a foundational understanding of Zoroastrianism.

Carrithers, Michael. *Buddha: A Very Short Introduction.* Oxford: Oxford University Press, 1996. In just over 100 pages, Carrithers manages to provide a compelling account of the Buddha's life and teaching. The book is especially good at situating the Buddha in the cultural context of the Gangetic basin during India's "second urbanization."

Dawson, Raymond, trans. *The Analects.* Oxford: Oxford University Press, 1993. A very good recent English translation of the *Analects*.

Dundas, Paul. *The Jains*, 2nd ed. London and New York: Routledge, 2002. A thorough, scholarly introduction to the history of Jainism. Probably the best available introduction to the religion.

Foltz, Richard C. *Spirituality in the Land of the Noble: How Iran Shaped the World's Religions.* Oxford: Oneworld Publications, 2004. This very readable book is helpful in understanding the characteristics of Indo-Iranian religion, the reforms of Zoroaster, and the subsequent effects of Zoroastrianism on other religions. It also explores the Buddhist presence in Iran and the changes brought by the advent of Islam to the region.

Hopkins, Thomas J. *The Hindu Religious Tradition*. Belmont, CA: Wadsworth Publishing, 1971. This brief text is one of the clearest presentations of basic Hinduism in English. It is especially good for understanding the Vedic and classical periods in Hinduism. Highly recommended as a short, comprehensive study of Hinduism.

Ivanhoe, Philip J. *Confucian Moral Self Cultivation*, 2nd ed. Indianapolis: Hackett Publishing Company, 2000. A compact book by one of the leading contemporary scholars of classical Chinese philosophy, this text focuses on one of the salient themes of early Confucianism. It also provides useful chapters on both Mencius and Xunzi.

———, trans. *The Daodejing of Laozi*. New York: Seven Bridges Press, 2002. Many English translations of the Daodejing are available, but I believe this is one of the best. It is very readable yet preserves the elusive and evocative quality of the original text.

Jaspers, Karl. *The Origin and Goal of History*. Michael Bullock, trans. New Haven: Yale University Press, 1953. This is the book that introduced the concept of the Axial Age, but it is about more than just the Axial period. It is Jaspers's comprehensive philosophy of history, developed in a deliberate attempt to avoid the Eurocentrism that characterized earlier efforts in the sub-discipline. Unfortunately, the book is difficult to find nowadays.

Mair, Victor H., trans. *Wandering on the Way: Early Taoist Tales and Parables of Chuang Tzu*. New York: Bantam Books, 1994. Because the Zhuangzi has not been translated into English with the same frequency as the Daodejing, there are not as many versions to choose from. Among the translations of the last few decades, I prefer Mair's. His is one of the few complete English translations of the Zhuangzi, and it is accessible to the general reader.

Mascaró, Juan, trans. *The Upanishads*. Baltimore: Penguin Books, 1965. Although not as accurate or as elegant as later translations, Mascaró's rendering is very accessible and readily available in the Penguin Classics edition. Represents a good selection of the most significant Upanishads.

Poo, Mu-Chou. *In Search of Personal Welfare: A View of Ancient Chinese Religion*. Albany: State University of New York Press, 1998. Focuses on the "popular" religion of early China and its continuities and discontinuities with "official" religion.

Rahula, Walpola. *What the Buddha Taught*. New York: Grove Press, 1959. Walpola Rahula was a Sri Lankan monk from the Theravada tradition, the oldest extant Buddhist tradition. His book, published in 1959, remains one of the best introductions to the Four Noble Truths in English. Highly recommended.

Sharma, Arvind. *Classical Hindu Thought: An Introduction*. New Delhi: Oxford University Press, 2000. Sharma's book is one of the clearest expositions available of the fundamental concepts in classical Hinduism. Each chapter is devoted to a particular idea, such as karma or *moksha*, which allows the reader to rapidly find the subject of his or her interest. The Introduction provides a helpful overview of Hindu thought, showing the relationship of Niguna Brahman and Saguna Brahman theologies.

Supplementary Reading:

Basham, A. L. *The Origin and Development of Classical Hinduism*. New York: Oxford University Press, 1995. This book covers much of the same material as *The Wonder That Was India* (below) but in far less detail. It is a clear account of the Axial Age developments that gave rise to Hinduism. Makes a good introduction to the study of Hinduism from a historical perspective.

———. *The Wonder That Was India*. New York: Grove Press, 1959. A classic presentation of the history of Indian culture from the earliest times through the first millennium C.E.

Berthrong, John H., and Evelyn Nagai Berthrong. *Confucianism: A Short Introduction*. Oxford: Oneworld Publications, 2000. A readable overview of Confucianism. The introduction follows an imaginary Confucian family of 17th-century China through a typical day. Useful for understanding the development of post-Axial Confucianism.

Bodhi, Bhikkhu, trans. *In the Buddha's Words: An Anthology of Discourses from the Pali Canon (Teachings of the Buddha)*. Boston: Wisdom Publications, 2005. This is a selection of previously published translations of Suttas in the Pali Canon. Bhikkhu Bodhi, a Theravadin monk, is a fine translator. The collection provides a representative selection of all the Sutta collections in the Pali Canon. If you are interested in reading the earliest Buddhist scriptures in English translation, this is a good place to begin.

———. *The Noble Eightfold Path: Way to the End of Suffering*. Seattle: BPS Pariyatti Editions, 1994. The casual reader may find this presentation of the Buddha's Noble Path a bit dry, but it details about as clearly as possible the spiritual discipline leading to *nibbana* as it was most probably practiced by early Buddhists.

Brereton, Joel. "The Upanishads." In *Approaches to the Asian Classics*, edited by Wm. Theodore de Bary and Irene Bloom. New York: Columbia University Press, 1990. This essay discusses the major themes of the Upanishads and provides a useful introduction to Upanishadic theology and mysticism.

Brooks, E. Bruce, and A. Taeko Brooks. *The Original Analects: Sayings of Confucius and His Successors*. New York: Columbia University Press, 1998. One of the controversial new works in Confucian studies, which reduces Confucius's contribution to the *Analects* to a part of chapter 4. The rest, the authors argue, was composed over a period of two centuries by followers with a very different philosophical outlook from the sage himself.

Collins, Stevens. *Selfless Persons: Imagery and Thought in Theravada Buddhism*. Cambridge: Cambridge University Press, 1982. This well-written book is an impressive piece of scholarship. Definitely not an introductory work, it is perhaps the best exposition of no-self I've read.

Dhamma, Rewata. *The First Discourse of the Buddha*. Boston: Wisdom Publications, 1997. An introductory exposition of basic Buddhist concepts and the Four Noble Truths, written by a scholarly Theravadin monk from Myanmar.

Eck, Diana L. *Darśan: Seeing the Divine Image in India*, 2nd ed., rev. and enl. Chambersburg, PA: Anima Books, 1985. A wonderful, succinct study of the role of images in popular Hinduism. Insightful and accessible to non-specialists.

Edgerton, Franklin. *The Beginnings of Indian Philosophy*. Cambridge, MA: Harvard University Press, 1965. A scholarly presentation of the origins of Hindu philosophy, with thoughtful translations of Vedic hymns and early Upanishads.

Eisenstadt, S. N., ed. *The Origins and Diversity of Axial Age Civilizations*. Albany: State University of New York Press, 1986. An informative collection of essays on the Axial Age transformations in ancient Judah, Greece, India, and China, mainly from sociological points of view. Eisenstadt's introductions are especially helpful. This is one of the very few scholarly texts that exclusively treat the Axial Age.

Fairservis, Walter A., Jr. *The Roots of Ancient India*, 2nd ed., rev. Chicago: University of Chicago Press, 1975. This is one of the best scholarly analyses of the Indus Valley civilization.

Feuerstein, Georg, Subhash Kak, and David Frawley. *In Search of the Cradle of Civilization: New Light on Ancient India*. Wheaton, IL, and Chennai, India: Quest Books, 1995, 2001. This collaborative work challenges the Aryan "invasion theory" and advances the argument that Indus and Aryan cultures have always been one.

Fingarette, Herbert. *Confucius: The Secular as Sacred.* New York: Harper Torchbooks, 1972. Fingarette offers a thoughtful reading of Confucius that attempts to show his relevance for modern life by emphasizing the importance of rituals in daily life. This text is not one to *begin* a study of Confucius, but it is a provocative interpretation for those who have a basic understanding of the Chinese sage.

Fronsdal, Gil, trans. *Dhammapada: A New Translation of the Buddhist Classic with Annotations*. Boston: Shambhala, 2005. The *Dhammapada* is a Buddhist favorite. It is a slim collection of short verses taken from various places in the tradition. Fronsdal's is a very good recent translation.

Fung, Yu-Lan. *A History of Chinese Philosophy*. Vol. 1: *The Period of the Philosophers*. Princeton: Princeton University Press, 1952. This work is a classic. It was first published in the 1930s, but it still ranks as an excellent introduction to philosophical thought in the late Chinese Axial Age. The book is principally written to philosophers and scholars and, thus, assumes some familiarity with the discipline.

Graham, A. C. *Disputers of the Dao: Philosophical Argument in Ancient China.* Chicago and La Salle, IL: Open Court Publishing Company, 1989. Graham's work, like Fung's, is also written for scholars. Many non-specialists may find the book a bit obscure and hard to read, but this is an important analysis of early Chinese philosophy.

Gunaratana, Henepola. *Mindfulness in Plain English*, expanded and updated ed. Boston: Wisdom Publications, 2002. If you are interested in the practice of Buddhist *vipassana* meditation, there is no better book with which to start. Highly recommended.

Hamilton, Sue. *Indian Philosophy: A Very Short Introduction.* Oxford: Oxford University Press, 2001. The "Very Short Introduction" series by Oxford University Press contains several excellent works on Asian religions and philosophies. This slim volume provides a good overview of the basic presuppositions of Indian thought and the various schools that developed in Indian history. Makes a good introduction to the study of Indian philosophy.

Harrapa. Harappa.com, 1995–2006. www.harappa.com/. This well-designed Web site contains hundreds of pictures of artifacts and ruins from the ancient civilization, as well as some excellent articles explaining them. There is even an online store for purchasing coffee mugs, T-shirts, and other items featuring Indus images.

Harvey, Peter. *An Introduction to Buddhism: Teachings, History, and Practices*. Cambridge: Cambridge University Press, 1990. This is one of the best comprehensive introductions to Buddhism. It begins with the life and teachings of the Buddha and traces the development of the three major forms of Buddhism, clearly delineating their characteristic features.

Hick, John. *An Interpretation of Religion: Human Responses to the Transcendent*, 2nd ed. New Haven and London: Yale University Press, 1989, 1991, 2004. In this wide-ranging theological work, John Hick, a prominent contemporary Protestant theologian, tries to show that the world's post-Axial religions are united in their endeavor to reorient their adherents from self-centeredness to reality-centeredness. In making his case, Hick spends several chapters discussing the characteristics of Axial Age religions and distinguishing them from pre-Axial religious forms. Whether or not one agrees with Hick's overall argument, the book is useful in the way it marshals evidence and texts from many traditions to show the change in religious function prompted by the Axial Age.

Hultgård, Anders. "Persian Apocalypticism." In *The Continuum History of Apocalypticism*, edited by Bernard J. McGinn, John J. Collins, and Stephen J. Stein, pp. 30–63. New York and London: Continuum, 2003. A scholarly and technical study of the influence of Zoroastrianism on the religions of Semitic origin.

Hume, Robert Ernest, trans. *The Thirteen Principal Upanishads*, 2nd rev. ed. New York: Oxford University Press, 1971. Hume's translation is one of the relatively early English translations of the Upanishads. After more than a century, it is still one of the best and most scholarly. The introduction and textual notes are very helpful.

Huyler, Stephen P. *Meeting God: Elements of Hindu Devotion*. New Haven and London: Yale University Press, 1999. This is a beautiful book. Its well-written text is supplemented by rich images of Hindu piety. Highly recommended for understanding Hindu iconography and worship.

Ivanhoe, Philip J., and Bryan W. Van Norden. *Readings in Classical Chinese Philosophy.* New York: Seven Bridges Press, 2001. This is an excellent anthology, containing excerpts from many of the important philosophical works produced during the Chinese Axial Age. Among the works it includes are selections from the *Analects*, the Mencius, the Xunzi, the Zhuangzi, and the complete Ivanhoe translation of the Daodejing. The best text of its kind.

Jaini, Padmanabh S. *The Jaina Path of Purification.* Delhi: Motilal Banarsidass Publishers Pvt. Ltd., 1998. A classic introduction to the religion by a scholar who is a practicing Jain.

Jensen, Lionel. *Manufacturing Confucianism: Chinese Traditions and Universal Civilization*. Durham, NC: Duke University Press, 1997. One of the controversial pieces of new scholarship in Confucian studies. As the title of his book implies, Jensen claims that Confucianism was largely the product of later Confucianists and others, rather than the development of the teachings of a historical sage named Confucius.

Klostermaier, Klaus. *A Survey of Hinduism*. Albany: State University Press of New York, 1991. An eminently readable and comprehensive study of Hinduism in all its major dimensions. Highly recommended.

Kohn, Livia, and Michael LaFargue, eds. *Lao Tzu and the Tao-te-ching.* Albany: State University of New York Press, 1998. A scholarly collection of essays on early Daoism, focusing on the myth of Laozi and the interpretation of the Daodejing in China and in the West.

Koller, John M. *Asian Philosophies*, 4th ed. Upper Saddle River, NJ: Prentice Hall, 2002. I use this textbook in my course on Asian Philosophy. It is one of the clearest presentations of the basic philosophies of India and China in a single volume. Here, you will find not only the classical-era philosophies of Asia but also other perspectives, such as Islam, Neo-Confucianism, and modern developments in Hinduism and Buddhism. This is a good resource for getting a foundational perspective on the many Asian worldviews. Because this is a secondary source, it should be read in conjunction with the primary texts from each tradition.

Lau, D. C., trans. *The Analects*. London: Penguin Books Ltd., 1979. An excellent translation of the Confucian classic. The introduction is especially good.

———, trans. *Mencius*. London: Penguin Books Ltd., 1970. Lau is one of the best contemporary translators of the ancient Chinese texts.

Mahony, William K. *The Artful Universe: An Introduction to the Vedic Religious Imagination*. Albany: State University of New York Press, 1998. A skillful interpretation of the world of the Veda, focusing on the interconnections of language, ritual, and nature. Some excellent translations of key Vedic texts.

Mair, Victor H., trans. *Tao Te Ching*. New York: Bantam Books, 1990. Another fine translation of the Daoist classic.

Malandra, William W., trans. and ed. *An Introduction to Ancient Iranian Religion: Readings from the Avesta and Achaemenid Inscriptions*. Minneapolis: University of Minnesota Press, 1983. A translation of the Avesta and other early Zoroastrian writings, with useful introductory material.

McCutcheon, Russell T., ed. *The Insider/Outsider Problem in the Study of Religion: A Reader*. London: Cassell Academic Press, 1998. This is an important recent collection of essays exploring various aspects of the methodologies of religious studies.

Miller, Barbara Stoler, trans. *The Bhagavad-Gita: Krishna's Counsel in Time of War*. New York: Bantam Books, 1986. One of the best English translations available. I use Miller's version of the Gita for my undergraduate courses.

Miller, James. *Daoism: A Short Introduction*. Oxford: Oneworld Publications, 2003. A comprehensive introduction to Daoism, focused on its religious manifestations.

Mitchell, Robert Allen. *The Buddha: His Life Retold*. New York: Paragon House, 1989. This is a lively retelling of the Buddha's life drawn from a wide range of sources, including the mythological accounts. For contrast, consult Bhikkhu Ñanamoli's *The Life of the Buddha*.

Ñanamoli, Bhikkhu. *The Life of the Buddha: According to the Pali Canon*, new ed. Seattle: Pariyatti Publishing, 2001. This is the only account of the Buddha's life (that I am aware of) that solely uses the Pali Canon as its source. The text of Bhikkhu Ñanamoli's work is essentially long passages from the Pali Canon connected by narrative comments. For contrast, consult Robert Allen Mitchell's *The Buddha: His Life Retold.*

———, and Bhikkhu Bodhi. *The Middle Length Discourses of the Buddha: A Translation of the Majjhima Nikaya (Teachings of the Buddha)*, new ed. Boston: Wisdom Publications, 1995. For someone deeply interested in Buddhism, there is no substitute for reading the Suttas themselves. The Middle-Length Discourses is my recommendation as the place to start.

Nelson, Walter Henry. *Buddha, His Life and His Teachings.* New York: Jeremy P. Tarcher/Putnam, 1996. A biography of the Buddha and an introduction to his teachings for the non-specialist. Very accessible.

Obeyesekere, Gananath. *Imagining Karma: Ethical Transformations in Amerindian, Buddhist, and Greek Rebirth.* Berkeley and Los Angeles: University of California Press, 2002. Obeyesekere's work is an impressive volume exploring the conceptualization of rebirth and karma in a variety of cultural contexts. It is useful both for its comparative analysis and its explanation of how rebirth came to be ethicized and connected to the doctrine of karma in the South Asian Axial Age.

O'Flaherty, Wendy D., ed. *Karma and Rebirth in Classical Indian Traditions*. Berkeley, CA: University of California Press, 1980. This work is a collection of essays by leading Indologists on the development of the concepts of transmigration and karma in the classical period.

———, trans. *The Rig-Veda: An Anthology*. Harmondsworth, Middlesex, England: Penguin Books, 1981. A compelling selection and translation of the most interesting Rig Veda texts. This anthology is an essential resource for the non-specialist interested in a deeper understanding of the Vedic period.

Oldstone-Moore, Jennifer. *Taoism*. Oxford and New York: Oxford University Press, 2003. A good, succinct academic introduction to Daoism, focused mainly on its later history.

Olivelle, Patrick, trans. *Upaniśads*. Oxford: Oxford University Press, 1996. Olivelle's translation is a superb rendering for the modern reader. It is informed by careful scholarship and provides excellent introductory material. This is the best of recent translations.

Panikkar, Raimundo. *The Vedic Experience: Mantramanjari.* Los Angeles: University of California Press, 1977. Panikkar's collection is an assembly of more than 500 Vedic texts translated into vigorous and compelling English.

Radhakrishnan, Sarvepalli, and Charles A. Moore, eds. *A Sourcebook in Indian Philosophy*. Princeton: Princeton University Press, 1967. A fine selection of important Hindu texts, this work includes primary sources from the six orthodox schools of Hindu philosophy, as well as texts from the heterodox traditions.

Smith, Wilfred Cantwell. *The Meaning and End of Religion*. New York: MacMillan and Company, 1963 (reprinted by Augsburg Fortress Publishers, 1991). Smith has written an impressive account of the history of the *concept* of religion and a provocative argument against its uncritical usage. This is a good work for understanding why religion is such a difficult—perhaps impossible—phenomenon to define.

Tatia, Nathmal, trans. *That Which Is: Tattvārtha Sūtra*. San Francisco: HarperCollins Publishers, 1994. An English translation of one of the earliest Jain texts, recognized as authoritative by different Jain sects. It provides information on the Jain view of the cosmos, humanity, and the path to liberation. Helpful introductory material.

Thompson, Laurence G. *Chinese Religion: An Introduction*. Belmont, CA: Dickenson Publishing Co., 1969. Part of the "Religious Life in History" series (which also contains Thomas J. Hopkin's introduction to Hinduism), this short text offers a comprehensive overview of religion in China.

Tu, Weiming and Mary Evelyn Tucker, eds. *Confucian Spirituality*. Vol. 1. New York: Crossroad Publishing Company, 2003. I like this book very much. It opened my eyes to the spiritual dimensions of Confucianism and helped me to appreciate Confucian thought and practice in an entirely new way. The text is an anthology of essays by leading scholars of Confucian studies.

Van Norden, Bryan W., ed. *Confucius and the Analects: New Essays*. Oxford and New York: Oxford University Press, 2002. This is a collection of essays by a wide range of scholars—some sinologists, some philosophers—on Confucius and the principal source of information about him, the *Analects*. This anthology is both accessible to the educated reader and representative of fine scholarship in Confucian studies.

Waley, Arthur. *Three Ways of Thought in Ancient China*. Stanford, CA: Stanford University Press, 1982. Waley's book has become a classic study of early Chinese philosophy. Written in the 1930s, the book is still used as an introduction to Chinese thought in some university and college courses. It focuses on Mencius, Zhuangzi, and Realism/Legalism. Elegantly written.

Watson, Burton, trans. *Xunzi: Basic Writings*. New York: Columbia University Press, 2003. A recent reissue of an older translation, this is the most accessible version of the Xunzi for the non-specialist.

———, trans. Zhuangzi*: Basic Writings*. New York: Columbia University Press, 2003. Another good translation of the Zhuangzi, although not the complete text.

Wheeler, Mortimer. *Civilizations of the Indus Valley and Beyond*. New York: McGraw-Hill, 1972. Wheeler's writings on the Indus Valley provide a wealth of information. This work focuses on the archaeology of the Indus Valley and northern Indian culture up to the Mauryan Empire.

Internet Resources:

Access to Insight. www.accesstoinsight.org/. This is an excellent Web site for studying the earliest texts of Buddhism. Contains English translations of texts from the Pali Canon and links to the Canon itself, study guides, and helpful information about Theravada Buddhism.

Avesta.org. www.avesta.org/. This Web site contains many useful resources for understanding Zoroastrianism, including translations of the Avesta and other Zoroastrian texts, glossaries, calendars, explanations of rituals, and many interpretive essays.

Bodhi, Bhikkhu. *The Noble Eightfold Path: Way to the End of Suffering*. Seattle: BPS Pariyatti Editions, 1994. Available free online at www.vipassana.com/ resources/8fp0.php. For annotation, see above.

BuddhaNet. Buddha Dharma Education Association, Inc./BuddhaNet, 1992–2006. www.buddhanet.net/. A comprehensive Web site with material on all Buddhist traditions throughout the world.

ConfucianStudies.com. ConfucianStudies.com., 2004. www.confucianstudies.com/. A Web site that serves as a clearinghouse for students and scholars of Confucianism and other aspects of Chinese thought and religion. Here, you will find links to articles, lists of Confucian scholars, and other resources for the study of the tradition.

Jinavani.com. Jinvani Systech Pvt. Ltd., India. www.jinvani.com/. A Web site maintained by Jains in India that provides information on Jain philosophy, history, and news relevant to the modern Jain community.

Kenoyer, Jonathan Mark. "Mohenjo-daro!" Harappa.com, 2005. www.mohenjodaro.net/. This site contains more than 100 images from Mohenjo-daro, one of two principal cities of the Indus culture. There is a slide show, an introductory essay, and links to other interesting sites.

Vipassana Fellowship. www.vipassana.com. A nice Web site focused on the Buddhist meditation practice called *vipassana*, or "insight." The site contains instructions on how to meditate, as well as links to many other useful resources in Theravada Buddhism.

The World of Traditional Zoroastrianism. www.zoroastrianism.com/. This Web site is maintained by traditional Mazdayasni Zarathushtris and provides a glimpse of contemporary Zoroastrianism from within the tradition itself.

Notes